Match of My Life

DERBY
COUNTY

KNOW THE SCORE BOOKS PUBLICATIONS

CULT HEROES	Author	ISBN
CARLISLE UNITED	Mark Harrison	978-1-905449-09-7
CHELSEA	Leo Moynihan	1-905449-00-3
MANCHESTER CITY	David Clayton	978-1-905449-05-7
NEWCASTLE	Dylan Younger	1-905449-03-8
NOTTINGHAM FOREST	David McVay	978-1-905449-06-4
RANGERS	Paul Smith	978-1-905449-07-1
SOUTHAMPTON	Jeremy Wilson	1-905449-01-1
WEST BROM	Simon Wright	1-905449-02-X

MATCH OF MY LIFE	Editor	ISBN
ENGLAND WORLD CUP	Massarella & Moynihan	1-905449-52-6
EUROPEAN CUP FINALS	Ben Lyttleton	1-905449-57-7
FA CUP FINALS 1953-1969	David Saffer	978-1-905449-53-8
FULHAM	Michael Heatley	1-905449-51-8
LEEDS	David Saffer	1-905449-54-2
LIVERPOOL	Leo Moynihan	1-905449-50-X
MANCHESTER UNITED	Ivan Ponting	978-1-905449-59-0
SHEFFIELD UNITED	Nick Johnson	1-905449-62-3
STOKE CITY	Simon Lowe	978-1-905449-55-2
SUNDERLAND	Rob Mason	1-905449-60-7
SPURS	Allen & Massarella	978-1-905449-58-3
WOLVES	Simon Lowe	1-905449-56-9

GENERAL FOOTBALL	Author	ISBN
2007/08 CHAMPIONS LEAGUE YEARBOOK		978-1-905449-93-4
BURKSEY	Peter Morfoot	1-905449-49-6
The Autobiography of a Football God		
HOLD THE BACK PAGE	Harry Harris	1-905449-91-7
MARTIN JOL: The Inside Story	Harry Harris	978-1-905449-77-4
MY PREMIERSHIP DIARY	Marcus Hahnemann	978-1-905449-33-0
Reading's Season in the Premiership		
OUTCASTS	Steve Menary	978-1-905449-31-6
The Lands That FIFA Forgot		
PARISH TO PLANET	Eric Midwinter	978-1-905449-30-9
A History of Football		
2006 WORLD CUP DIARY	Harry Harris	1-905449-90-9

| TACKLES LIKE A FERRET (England Cover) | Paul Parker | 1-905449-47-X |
| TACKLES LIKE A FERRET (Manchester United Cover) | Paul Parker | 1-905449-46-1 |

CRICKET	Author	ISBN
MOML: THE ASHES	Pilger & Wightman	1-905449-63-1
GROVEL! The 1976 West IndiesTour of England	David Tossell	978-1-905449-43-9
MY AUTOBIOGRAPHY	Shaun Udal	978-1-905449-42-2
WASTED?	Paul Smith	978-1-905449-45-3
LEAGUE CRICKET YEARBOOK North West edition	Andy Searle	978-1-905449-70-5
LEAGUE CRICKET YEARBOOK Midlands edition	Andy Searle	978-1-905449-72-9

RUGBY LEAGUE	Editor	ISBN
MOML: WIGAN WARRIORS	David Kuzio	978-1-905449-66-8

FORTHCOMING PUBLICATIONS

CULT HEROES	Author	ISBN
CELTIC	David Potter	978-1-905449-08-8

MATCH OF MY LIFE	Editor	ISBN
ASTON VILLA	Neil Moxley	978-1-905449-65-1
BOLTON WANDERERS	David Saffer	978-1-905449-64-4

Match of My Life

DERBY COUNTY

Editor: Nick Johnson
Series Editor: Simon Lowe

www.knowthescorebooks.com

First published in the United Kingdom
by Know The Score Books Limited, 2007

Know The Score Books Limited
118 Alcester Road
Studley
Warwickshire
B80 7NT
01527 454482
info@knowthescorebooks.com

www.knowthescorebooks.com

A CIP catalogue record is available for this book from the British Library
ISBN: 978-1-905449-68-2

Jacket and book design by Lisa David

Printed and bound in Great Britain by William Clowes Ltd, Beccles, Suffolk

Front cover:
Top left: The 1971/72 Championship-winning team show off their silverware.
Bottom left: Michael Johnson lifts the 2007 Play-off trophy.
Bottom right: Dean Sturridge and Marco Gabbiadini celebrate promotion in 1996.

Rear cover:
Top left: The 1946 FA Cup-winning team with the famous old trophy.
Top right: Kevin Wilson; 1980s goalscorer supreme.
Bottom: Darren Moore celebrates promotion in 2007.

Lots of love to my
darling Maria

Editor's Acknowledgements

Sincere thanks first of all go to the past and present players who generously gave up their time to be interviewed for this book. All 14 readily agreed to my request and their co-operation is greatly appreciated.

I am grateful to Roy McFarland for providing the foreword to the book. Roy features prominently in the history of Derby County and clearly has a great deal of affection for the club, so I was delighted when he accepted my invitation to say a few words.

The following people deserve praise for helping to put me in touch with interviewees: Roger Davies, Matt Reeder (media officer, Derby County FC), Colin Wood (communications manager, Sheffield Wednesday FC), Ian Hayes (www.derbycounty-mad.co.uk), Phil Matthews (reporter, Ram FM) and Eddie Greenhough.

I referred to Gerald Mortimer's book, Derby County: The Complete Record (Breedon Books), which proved to be an excellent source of facts and figures relating to the club. Club historian Mike Wilson and Paul Days, who is a member of the Association of Football Statisticians, also supplied some valuable information.

For providing inspiration and sharing memories of their experiences, I'd like to mention the following Derby supporters, who I know personally: Ian Cameron, Les Cowley, Loz Hunt, Michael L Kitsull, Mark Marriott, Nigel Scattergood, Steve Wallis, Stuart Wilson and Barrie Wild.

Finally, thanks go to my publisher, Simon Lowe of Know The Score Books, for giving me the opportunity to write this book.

Nick Johnson
October 2007

Contents

Introduction

It was a pleasure to speak to 14 past and current players about their time at Derby County for this book, which is my second title in the Match of My Life series. All the people I interviewed have interesting stories to tell from the memorable matches they played in, as well as being able to give an insight into the personalities involved with the club.

The matches featured span over sixty years, from victory over Charlton in the 1946 FA Cup final to the Play-off final win against West Brom at the end of the 2006/07 season, which saw Derby return to the Premiership in Billy Davies' first season in charge.

Jim Bullions recalls that fateful day at Wembley in 1946 when the Rams won the Cup for the first time. Reg Harrison, who is the only other surviving member of the Cup-winning side, reflects on a memorable match against Arsenal in which he scored the winning goal. Johnny Morris, who himself had won the FA Cup with Manchester United in 1948, casts his mind back to 1949 when he scored a hat-trick against Stoke on the last day of the season and Bert Mozley recollects a remarkable clash with Sunderland a year later which produced 11 goals.

Keith Havenhand goes back to the 1961/62 season when he achieved the rare feat of scoring two hat-tricks against the same club. Dave MacKay, whose arrival at the club heralded the start of Derby's unprecedented success under Brian Clough, reminisces about a fine victory over his former club Spurs at the end of the decade. Steve Powell remembers playing in a crucial game against Liverpool when he was just 16 which virtually sealed Derby's first Football League championship. The following season, the Rams secured a famous FA Cup victory at Tottenham and Roger Davies discusses his match-winning contribution in that game.

Of course winning trophies means Europe and Peter Daniel talks about the dramatic UEFA Cup win over Atletico Madrid during 1974/75, a season in which he stepped out of the shadows to play a key role in Derby's second Championship success.

Legendary Rams striker Kevin Wilson gives his thoughts on a fine solo display in 1984 when he scored four goals in a League Cup match and the 1986/87 Second Division title-winning campaign is covered by Phil Gee who scored the winner in a crucial game towards the end of that season. Another striker, 'Magic' Marco Gabbiadini, picks out a memorable win over his former club Sunderland during the 1995/96 promotion-winning season.

No collection of memorable Derby matches would be complete without the inclusion of a victory over arch-rivals Forest and that is taken care of by long-serving defender Michael Johnson, who nominated a crucial 4-2 win against them in 2004. The book concludes where it started – with success at Wembley, albeit the new model, with Darren Moore's account of the win over West Brom in the 2007 Championship Play-off final, which took the Rams back to the Premiership after a five-year absence.

I enjoyed hearing the stories and re-living some of the great moments in the proud history of Derby County. I hope you find the book to be an interesting read.

Nick Johnson
October 2007

Foreword

I had no hesitation in accepting a request to write the foreword to this book because Derby County Football Club has been a major a major part of my life. I started out at Tranmere Rovers, but I've almost been a one-club player because I spent the majority of my career at Derby and I was happy to stay. My association with the club – as a player, coach and manager – adds up to about 27 years. It's been a roller-coaster ride, but it's been magnificent.

When I signed for Derby I never expected things to turn out the way they did. Within a few years, we were playing in the First Division and then competing for the title, which we of course then won in the 1971/72 season. Brian Clough and Peter Taylor, as a managerial duo, brought the team together and performed miracles, so it was a magical time. It was the signing of Dave MacKay, who is featured in this book, which really set the whole place buzzing. He was a Scotland international who'd done the League and Cup 'double' with Spurs and when he walked through the door, the majority of us younger players felt that things were going to happen. And things did happen. In Dave we had a leader we all wanted to follow. By the time he left the likes of Colin Todd and Archie Gemmill were on board and we took the next step, winning the First Division. We felt as if we'd taken the club a stage further by winning the Championship because that had never happened before.

When Clough and Taylor came to the club all Derby really had in terms of recognition was that they'd won the FA Cup just after the war. They managed to mould a Championship-winning side, which is the ultimate accolade for a club because it's the hardest thing to win. Three years later, we won the Championship again. I missed most of that season through injury and my deputy, Peter Daniel, did a magnificent job while I was out, which he talks about here. I watched the majority of the games and Colin Todd also shouldered a lot of the responsibility in defence during my absence showing what a great player he was.

We also had some memorable nights at the Baseball Ground when we played in the European Cup and reached the semi-finals of the competition. They are memories that will live forever in the minds of the players and supporters who experienced them. There were one or two sad times along the way, such as losing to Manchester United in the semi-finals of the FA Cup, but football is about the highs and the lows.

Although I'm a Liverpool lad, I really count Derbyshire as my home. It didn't take me long to settle in the area and since finishing playing, regardless of where I've coached or managed, I've always maintained my home in Derby. I've been at Bradford City, Bolton Wanderers, Cambridge United, Torquay United and Chesterfield, but I always kept my base in Derby because I always intended to stay in the area once I'd retired. My wife is from Derby and my daughter Beth, who's about to give birth to our first grandchild, was born in the city.

I can look back on some great times with Derby and I'm sure you'll enjoy recalling some of the memorable games in the history of the club.

Roy McFarland
October 2007

THE PLAYERS

JIM BULLIONS
WING-HALF 1944–1947

BORN   12 March 1924, Dennyloanhead
SIGNED   October 1944 from Chesterfield
RAMS CAREER   29 games, 0 goals
HONOURS   FA Cup winners medal 1946
LEFT   Transferred to Leeds United, November 1947; £2,000

Jim was raised in Derbyshire after moving from Scotland with his family at a young age. Having established himself in the Derby first team towards the end of the War, Jim was one of only three players who played in every round when Derby won the FA Cup in 1946. He and Reg Harrison are the two surviving members of the Cup-winning team and the pair remain in regular contact, attending games together at Pride Park.

Derby County 4 v Charlton Athletic 1

FA Cup final
Saturday 27 April 1946

Wembley Stadium
Attendance 98,215

Rams see off Addicks in extra-time to win Cup for the first time

Teams

Stuart McMillan	Managers	Jimmy Seed
Vic Woodley	1	Sam Bartram
Jack Nicholas	2	Harold Phipps
Jack Howe	3	Jack Shreeve
Jim Bullions	4	Bert Turner
Leon Leuty	5	John Oakes
Chick Musson	6	Bert Johnson
Reg Harrison	7	Leslie Fell
Raich Carter	8	Albert Brown
Jack Stamps	9	Arthur Turner
Peter Doherty	10	Don Welsh
Dally Duncan	11	Chris Duffy

B Turner (og) 85 Doherty 92 Stamps 97, 106	Scorers	B Turner 86

Referee: E Smith

FOOTBALL WAS IN MY blood. Born in Scotland, I was seven when my parents brought me and my two brothers down to England. My dad played amateur football and I've got the nine Scotland amateur international caps he won from 1909 to 1914.

Dad took me to see Derby play before the war, in 1938. They were a good side then, with the likes of Jack Nicholas, Sammy Crooks and Ronnie Dix among their number. When I was 15 war came. I was an apprentice surveyor at Oxcroft Colliery and I was playing for Shuttlewood, near Bolsover, in the Chesterfield Amateur League throughout the wartime. In the summer, we had a five-a-side competition in Shuttlewood and Bolsover and I got a team together. We won the final of the competition, which was played at Chesterfield's ground, Saltergate.

After playing for Clowne in the Worksop League, I went on to play for Chesterfield as an amateur against local teams such as Sheffield United, Sheffield Wednesday, Rotherham and Mansfield. They kept playing each other during the wartime because restrictions due to the lack of fuel meant they couldn't travel far. The authorities wanted football to continue as part of keeping the morale of the nation up, so organised regional leagues. I used to go to the match on the bus and ended up playing 20-odd games for Chesterfield as a right-half. One day I went into the dressing room and found that my boots weren't underneath my shirt. When I asked why they were missing, I was told to go and see the manager, Norman Bullock. I went into his office and said, "Mr Bullock, why aren't my boots underneath my shirt today?"

"Well, you're running about the field like a schoolboy," he replied. "I want you to come and sit with me in the stand."

I was heartbroken because my pals were coming to see me play. So I decided I wanted to go to a new club and there were scouts from Sheffield United, Sheffield Wednesday, Rotherham and Derby who came to watch me play. I picked Derby and the manager, Ted Magner, told me that I had to sign as a professional. "If you're an amateur, you could do the same to Derby as you did to Chesterfield," he said. I agreed to sign as a professional and got into the first-team straight away.

The War in Europe had ended and something like normality was resuming. So the 1945/46 season saw the FA Cup staged for the first time since Portsmouth beat Wolves 4-1 in 1939. And for the first time in the history of the competition, all ties were played over two legs. The idea was to make sure the massive crowds that were flocking to see football now that the hardship of the war was over could see as much as they wanted and with travel still being restricted having two legs meant that both sets of supporters had a home match in which to support their team.

Derby were fortunate that towards the end of the war we were able to secure the 'guest' services of two outstanding players, names that would forever become inseparable with the club's history: Raich Carter and Peter Doherty.

These were not normal times, you understand. For example, completely out of the blue, Carter, who was signed to Sunderland, had written to the club asking if he could play for us. Imagine the club's delight upon receiving this letter from the brilliant England international during the war. A telegram had been immediately dispatched to the RAF camp at Gloucester where Carter was stationed simply stating: "Yes please. As soon as you like."

Sometimes fortune smiles on you and she certainly did when another outstanding international inside-forward, Peter Doherty of Manchester City and Ireland, happened to be stationed even closer to the Baseball Ground at RAF Loughborough. The Irishman arrived at the RAF camp shortly after Carter had arranged to transfer to Loughborough from Gloucester. So now Derby had the two best inside-forwards in Britain 'guesting' for us.

The names of Carter and Doherty became synonymous with Derby County yet, surprisingly, their Rams' careers overlapped for only one official season and both had moved on within eighteen months.

When football began its first peacetime season for six years in 1945/46, both players were firmly established in the Derby team, although fortune continued to smile as, theoretically, the players' original clubs could recall them at any time. Fortunately for the Rams, Sunderland and Manchester City allowed both players to continue guesting for the Rams, who each felt that their 'parent' club had lost faith in them and so put everything into playing for us. Technically guests were only allowed to play in league games and both players put in transfer requests to move to Derby permanently. The then manager, Ted Magner, had plenty of hard bargaining to do, but managed to secure both players' transfers before the FA Cup deadline, although in the case of Carter's transfer there was a late scramble. After missing their connecting train, a late night taxi journey took Carter and Jack Catterall, the Derby secretary, from York to Sunderland. The paperwork was finally signed at 11pm, an hour before the FA Cup deadline, for a transfer fee of £6,000. It was not really a lot of money for such a wonderful player. Combined with the signing of Doherty, Ted Magner had probably pulled off probably the best piece of business the football club had ever transacted, so it was unfortunate that Ted left the club just as the Cup run started. Magner was a fine man. His man-management was superb. In fact he was a brilliant and vastly underrated boss. I don't want to take anything away from Stuart McMillan because he took us to Wembley after all. But it was Magner who fashioned the team.

WE STARTED THE competition with a comprehensive 9-0 win over Luton on aggregate and then we faced West Brom in the next round. We won the first leg 1-0 with a goal from the brilliant Peter Doherty, but he was missing for the second leg and all the newspaper reports said that we'd struggle without him. We were far from a one man team, though and Raich Carter wasn't having any of it. "I'll show 'em," he said to me. "You give me that ball." He was brilliant as we won 3-1 at the Hawthorns.

Raich used to take corners and free-kicks and he was a tremendous player. He was left-footed, so he demanded that the ball be played to his right side so that he could turn and hit it with his left foot. He didn't want it on his chest and he made that clear in no uncertain terms. I was the youngest in the team and Raich used to swear at me.

When we used to have team-talks, the older players took no notice of the younger ones like Reg Harrison and myself, who got called 'The Babes'. The likes of Carter, Doherty and Dally Duncan made all the decisions. When it came to my turn in one of the team-talks, new manager Stuart McMillan [appointed in the summer of 1945] would say, "What have you got to say for yourself, Jim?"

I remember once I said, "Well, when there's a corner kick, I've got the captain telling me to get in the penalty box. And when I get up there, I've got Raich Carter telling me to get back in my place."

"You've got to be diplomatic about it," McMillan replied, not helping me at all.

Raich didn't want to be told by the manager what to do because he knew that McMillan hadn't been much of a player. Ted Magner had been a good player. He used to put a ball down on the 18-yard line and could screw it into the net with either foot. When you've got somebody you can look up to as a manager, you take notice. Scotsman McMillan hadn't done much as a player in his time at Derby, Forest, Gillingham or Chelsea, so he let the senior players dominate.

Next we demolished Brighton 10-1 over the two legs, but met an altogether different proposition in Aston Villa in the quarter-final. We played out a fantastic game at Villa Park, winning 4-3, before holding on to a 1-1 draw at the Baseball Ground in a tense match that just saw us through.

Those wins over Brighton and Aston Villa set up a semi-final meeting with Birmingham. The semi-finals and final were to be one game only, but after drawing 1-1 at Hillsborough on the Saturday, we had to replay at Maine Road the following Wednesday. That game kicked off about two o'clock and there were loads of kids there who should have been at school. Their dads were passing them over the heads of supporters so they could stand at the front or sit on the wall. There were 80,000 fans there, probably mostly from Manchester just keen to see a top level game of football. I'd played well against Birmingham's inside-left at Hillsborough, but he nearly punished a mistake I made in the return game. He caught me in possession when I was dribbling, ran through on goal and only a good save from our goalkeeper Vic Woodley, who pushed the ball wide for a corner, prevented a goal. I wouldn't have been a hero if the ball had gone in then!

Vic was one of those players whose career was destroyed by the war. He had been a top notch goalkeeper in the 1930s with Chelsea, winning a then-record 19 England caps which was fabulous for a goalkeeper in those days when the selection committee kept chopping and changing people. By 1946 he was 36 years-old, which was veteran status even for goalkeepers back then. Players didn't tend to go on playing as long as they can now with all the fitness and dietary changes that have come in. Vic had played a couple of games for Chelsea, notably in the famous friendly game against Dynamo Moscow which over 80,000 people crammed into Stamford Bridge to watch. That was one of his last appearances for the Blues, though, because of his advancing years, and he was given a free transfer and ended up turning out for non-league Bath City. Strangely he only ended up at Derby because we had an injury crisis. Bill Townsed, our regular keeper, had injured himself just before the semi-final and MacMillan needed a quick fix. The manager gave Vic a call and he ended up filling the gap wonderfully. Vic actually only ever played 30 games for Derby, but one would be an FA Cup final!

Vic's save was a pivotal moment in the semi-final replay as we went on to win 4-0 and Birmingham finished the game with ten men because their right full-back broke his leg after tackling Peter Doherty in the build up to one of Doherty's two goals.

Doherty and Carter were brilliant together. We had a great forward line because Carter and Sammy Crooks were England internationals, Doherty played for Ireland and Dally Duncan was a Scotland player. Dally was a very good player. He was a proper wing-man who could go inside or outside and he had a knack of being able to cut across the ball and make it spin.

At the back, Leon Leuty was a good player who was unlucky not to get any recognition at international level. He didn't play for England because Neil Franklin of Stoke was in the side. Franklin won what was then a record 27 consecutive caps and made the centre-half position his own meaning Leon missed out.

GIVEN EVERYTHING THAT had happened since the 1939 Cup final – war, bombing, rationing, depravation and the loss of loved ones all over the country – the 1946 FA Cup final was the most eagerly anticipated of all Cup finals. It was just unbelievable that all the horrendous problems of war were over and crowds had flocked to enjoy football.

We travelled down south about a week before the Cup final and stayed at the Glen Eagles Hotel in Harpenden. There was a golf course nearby and Stuart McMillan was happy for us to play. Because there were no trolleys to use, players had to carry their clubs themselves or use a caddy. McMillan said that any players who didn't play golf had to caddy for someone else. I hadn't really played much golf by then, but Leon Leuty was a good golfer and I wasn't going to carry a big bag of clubs for him, so I decided to play. Sammy Crooks owned a sports shop in Derby along with a cricketer who played for Derbyshire and I went to Sammy's shop to buy some clubs before we travelled to Harpenden. That's when I really started to play golf. I can remember Sammy, who was a golf fanatic, driving the bus to the course.

There was actually a very real threat of the final not taking place. Some of the older players complained after learning that the seats allocated to their family members were out in the open. They were concerned that they'd get soaked if it rained, so they threatened to go on strike. Raich Carter represented the players and the matter was resolved amicably.

We travelled to Wembley in a Nottingham Council bus on the Wednesday before the match to take a look at the stadium and walk out onto the pitch. Sammy Chapman had been playing well before suffering an injury against Aston Villa in the fifth round. He couldn't play in the semi-final against Birmingham, but he returned for the League South fixture against Charlton a week before the final after clicking his knee back into place when he kicked a flat tyre on his car in frustration! He kept pestering the manager to play him at Wembley, but McMillan played Reg Harrison in his place. In those days, of course, there were no substitutes so you were either in or out. That was how it was and Reg was in and Sammy was out. It was tough to take.

There were only three of us who played in every round: Jack Nicholas, Raich Carter and myself. Jack Parr was a regular in the side all the way through the Cup run before breaking his arm guesting for Luton, forcing him to miss the final. Jack Howe, who had been abroad in the Army, came back in time to play at centre-half in the second semi-final against Birmingham and then switched to left-back to replace Parr in the final. And of course Vic had already come to the rescue in dramatic fashion.

WHEN THE MATCH kicked off at Wembley I can remember that my tongue was as dry as anything. The atmosphere had got to me and it wasn't until I touched the ball that I began to settle down and get into the game.

Reg Harrison fired in a good left-foot shot from the edge of the area which was turned over the bar by Sam Bartram before we took the lead. Stamps and Doherty were involved in the build-up and Dally Duncan's shot went in off defender Bert Turner. Duncan tried to claim the ball but it went down as an own-goal, which I'm sure Bert wasn't happy about.

Charlton equalised when Turner, who was their captain, took a free-kick which hit the inside of Peter Doherty's leg, throwing Woodley completely out. I think Woodley would have saved it had the ball not taken a deflection, but that was with just four minutes to go.

Jack Stamps, who was a big, burly centre-forward, had a chance to win the game for us in normal time when he hit the ball on the volley with the goal gaping, but, amazingly, it burst. I was behind him and I could see the ball deflating as it went through to the Charlton goalkeeper, Bartram. Straight away, Sam threw it out of the penalty area and I thought the referee would order a bounce-up on the goal-line. Instead, he took the ball outside the penalty area. The reason why he did that was because the ball wasn't the right size or weight by the time it got to Bartram, so therefore it had to be put in the place it had come from. It was the first time a ball had burst in a Cup Final. Amazingly, even though the authorities made a great play out of how good the newly-improved ball was, it burst again in the final at Wembley the following year when Charlton faced Burnley!

When we played extra-time, there were quite a few older players in the Charlton side. But as the youngest on the pitch, I was full of energy. I was full of myself, getting all over the field. I reckon I played better in that last half-an-hour than I did in the rest of the game.

In the early part of extra-time, we took the lead when Doherty followed up after Bartram parried a shot. Doherty then set up Stamps for a goal to put us 3-1 up and finally Stamps scored again. Jack had worked down the pit at Swinton, near Rotherham, and he and I were big pals.

I was able to shake hands with my dad and my mum's two sisters on my way up to collecting my medal from King George VI, but my mum was on her own in the stand opposite, sitting in a posh seat. I wasn't married then, so my mum and dad came down from Scotland with my two aunties to see me play.

I didn't celebrate winning the Cup by having a drink because I signed what they called 'The Pledge' when I was 12, agreeing to abstain from all intoxicating liquors, so I'm tee-total. I've never drunk in my life.

There was a parade when we got back to Derby a few days later, although there was no rest for us wicked. We'd had to reschedule our league match, at Southampton, for the Monday following the final. So the following day we arrived back in the city and went around the outskirts of Derby on a brewery wagon and thousands lined the streets. For a 22 year-old like me that was an incredible experience, made all the better by the knowledge that this was the first time the club had ever won the famous old trophy.

I LEFT DERBY TO join Leeds a year and a half after the Cup final. I'd lost my place in the side to Tim Ward, who'd been at Derby before the war. He and Stuart McMillan were friends and I thought there was some favouritism there because I felt I was playing good enough to be in the team. At Leeds I played with John Charles, who was younger than me, but we weren't hugely successful and it would take the arrival of Don Revie to turn them into a top club.

I made a lot more appearances for Derby than the record books show, but they didn't class wartime fixtures as competitive games so they were null and void.

My former Derby team-mate Sammy Crooks signed me for Shrewsbury from Leeds and I spent five years there. After playing for a few non-league clubs, I managed Alfreton Town in the Midland League and we won the Derby Senior Cup.

Away from football, I worked in the pit as a ventilation officer up until my retirement at the age of 60.

I played golf regularly until recently, usually with a number of old Derby players over the years, including Peter Cresswell, Ray Wilkins and Ray Young. But my knee has been giving me some problems lately, leading to a knee replacement which prevents me from playing at the moment.

We've lived at the same place near Staveley, on the outskirts of Chesterfield, for over fifty years. We bought a plot of land from the Duke of Devonshire for about £20 and then had a bungalow built on it. I still go to every home game with Reg Harrison and quite a few people still ask us to sign their autograph books and programmes. It was great to go back to Wembley for the Play-off final last season and it's great to see Derby in the Premiership.

It's amazing to think that it's over sixty years since we played there and won the Cup. I've got a copy of the Cup Final DVD, featuring interviews with Reg and I, which was produced not long ago. It's nice to be able to look back at what was a famous day in Derby's history.

REG HARRISON
RIGHT-WING 1944–1955

BORN   22 May 1923, Derby
SIGNED   March 1944 turned professional
RAMS CAREER   281 games, 59 goals
HONOURS   FA Cup winner 1946
LEFT   Transferred to Boston United, July 1955

Born and bred in Derby, Reg was 22 when he filled the number seven shirt vacated by the injured Sammy Crooks for the FA Cup Final against Charlton. Noted for his enthusiastic approach to the game, he remained with the Rams as the club's fortunes declined in the 1950s. After providing sterling service, Reg returned to haunt Derby as a member of the Boston side who pulled off a shock FA Cup win at the Baseball Ground.

Derby County 1 v Arsenal 0

League Division One
Saturday 29 November 1947

Baseball Ground
Attendance 35,713

A goal from Harrison ends Arsenal's 17-match unbeaten run

Teams

Stuart McMillan	**Managers**	Tom Whittaker
Bill Townsend	1	George Swindin
Bert Mozley	2	Lawrie Scott
Jack Howe	3	Walley Barnes
Tim Ward	4	Archie Macaulay
Leon Leuty	5	Les Compton
Chick Musson	6	Joe Mercer
Reg Harrison	7	Don Roper
Raich Carter	8	Reg Lewis
Angus Morrison	9	Ronnie Rooke
Billy Steel	10	James Logie
Allen Oliver	11	Ian McPherson
Harrison 32	**Scorer**	

Referee: T Smith

I WAS BORN in Normanton, but I lived at Chaddesdon from the age of two. I was a Derby fan and Sammy Crooks, Dally Duncan and Jack Bowers were my heroes, although I didn't go to many games as a kid because I always wanted to be playing myself.

During the war, I played for Derby Corinthians, who were the top amateur team in Derby at the time. It was funny; because of the Football League being suspended due to the hostilities, Sammy, Dally and Ralph Hann found themselves playing in the Derby Sunday League with us. They knew some of us showed some promise and so Sammy and Dally used to coach us while we were playing in games against each other and we were on the opposite side! If we did anything wrong, they'd tell us. They were absolutely great with us.

I signed for Derby at the age of 16 as an amateur and then war broke out. The club had a huge problem because the military requisitioned the Baseball Ground and so we had nowhere to play for quite some time. Eventually we ended up playing at the Municipal Sports Ground for a couple of years with skipper Jack Nicholas taking charge of pretty much everything to do with the club, organising us and the games and the kit. He did a great job. We eventually got back to the Baseball Ground and played our first game back there on Christmas Day 1942.

There were one or two clubs who were interested in signing me, including Sheffield United and Charlton. I was drafted into the Army and stationed at Chatham and a chap I was playing with down there told me he was going to become the manager of Gillingham. "Will you come with me when you get out?" he asked. I explained that I was still on Derby's books because they could retain you as an amateur during the war, so I couldn't sign for Gillingham. I was allowed, though, to guest for Hartlepools for a season and a half as my unit was then based up in the north east.

After writing a letter to Derby informing them that I was returning home on leave and would be available for a few games, I got home on the Thursday night and before I knew it Jack Nicholas, the Derby pre-war full-back and skipper who was acting as manager during most of the war, was round at our house. "You're playing for Derby reserves in the Bass Charity

Vase final at the Baseball Ground on Saturday," he said. They played me at centre-forward that day and I scored three goals. They signed me on as a professional the following day. I was later told it wasn't legal, signing someone on a Sunday, but I don't know if that was right. I played in the first-team the following week against Stoke, but my appearances were limited due to still being based up north.

WE BEGAN OUR campaign with a third round tie against Luton Town, winning 9-0 on aggregate (for the only time FA Cup ties were scheduled over two legs because of travel restrictions meaning that supporters found it very difficult to follow their team away from home). Then we beat West Brom 4-1, which was a fantastic result.

I missed a few games during the Cup run in 1946 because of being stationed at Lockerbie. After travelling from Scotland and getting into Derby at about one o'clock in the morning, then back on the bus again at nine o'clock to go down to Brighton to play, I would be absolutely shattered. After all the travelling, I asked Stuart McMillan, the manager, to be left out, so I missed the return game against Brighton and the two games against Aston Villa. I returned for the semi-final matches against Birmingham in place of the injured Sammy Crooks after being allowed home on leave. Following a 1-1 draw at Hillsborough, we played in front of a crowd of 80,000 at Maine Road, winning 4-0 in extra-time to secure our place in the final against Charlton.

Sammy took the injury extremely well considering. Before the game in Manchester, I was sat with him in the hotel and we talked for two hours, discussing football. What bloke would do that when you've taken his place? Dally was the same. Great blokes both of them.

I was never sure of playing in the final because Sammy declared himself fit as we prepared to play at Wembley. When we played Charlton the week before the final in a league game Sammy played outside-right and I played inside-right. Fortunately, the manager kept faith with me for the final, moving me out to the right wing, and I'm proud to have played in one of the most memorable games in Derby's history. Sammy wasn't so lucky, as Raich Carter came in to play at inside-right, I think because Stuart McMillan believed the Wembley turf would take its toll on his fitness.

It's true what they say, you don't remember much about playing in the Cup Final. However, I do recall something I said to the Queen Mother when we collected our winners' medals. "I bet it was warm out there," she said. "Aye," I replied, "it wor." Proper Derbyshire!

How about this for a run of fixtures: we played Charlton on the Saturday, Arsenal on the Monday and the Cup final on the Saturday. Then we played Southampton on the following Monday, Charlton on the Wednesday and Chelsea on the Saturday to complete our league programme. They wouldn't have that now!

Another way in which things are different concerns travelling to matches. When we travelled away, it was by coach unless we went to London, in which case we always went by train. I say we travelled by coach, but it was actually a bus which had been taken out of service. No tables and fridges like they have today – we certainly could never have imagined flying to a match, like Derby did to Plymouth recently!

Obviously winning the Cup final at Wembley is a very special moment, but as Jim Bullions had already been interviewed about the Cup triumph, I decided to select a memorable victory over Arsenal, when I scored the winner, for inclusion in this book as my Match of My Life. Arsenal then were a top team who'd gone 17 games unbeaten before playing us, so we did well to beat them. The Gunners side included Les Compton who was a great player, goalkeeper George Swindin, England forward Ronnie Rooke and Joe Mercer, who was a fabulous wing-half and would later win the title as manager of Manchester City and become caretaker-manager of England after Don Revie disappeared off to Saudi Arabia.

It should be said that we were on a good run ourselves, having gone two months and nine games unbeaten and we had won 1-0 at Highbury the previous season. On the Saturday before Arsenal visited us we won 5-1 at Charlton and so we were in terrific form.

In the first-half, Angus Morrison forced a great save out of George Swindin. Morrison was a workmanlike player who played as a centre-forward or on the left wing. He was one of the young lads at that time, like myself.

I scored what proved to be the winner just after the half-hour mark at the Normanton end of the ground. Allen Oliver sent the ball across from the left, Morrison couldn't get it and I knocked it in with my left shin. I've got a photo of the goal which shows Walley Barnes desperately trying to clear on the line as the ball crept just inside the post. Morrison is also in the photo, looking on. Barnes, who was a Wales international, was a bit annoyed and swore at me as the ball went in the net. He called me a "lucky so and so" because of the fact that I'd scored with my shin. "They all count," I replied.

Swindin had to make a several good saves as we tried to force a second goal. In our goal we had Bill Townsend, who was a good goalkeeper, but not outstanding. I was in the Army with him for six months at Lockerbie and we played football together there.

We were always reminded by the manager that when we went out on the pitch, we were all captains, so we had to do a certain amount of talking, but really Raich Carter was the boss because he commanded respect. His passing and positioning was excellent. I can't remember him doing much dribbling with the ball because it was all about passing. Raich was a dominant character on the field, but off it he was quite ordinary. Also in that side we had Jack Howe, who was the best footballer I've ever seen, I think. His kicking was so clean and he was the same with both feet.

Bert Mozley was a good player and I still speak to him regularly on the phone as he is now over in Canada. I also see his twin sister every week. I've known Bert since I was ten. Leon Leuty was a footballer; a good player and Tim Ward was a gentleman. Chick Musson was the hard man. He used to win the ball and give it to Raich or Peter Doherty before him. That was his job and he did it well. There wasn't any finesse about him. He just won the ball and left Raich or Peter to do the clever stuff.

I think inside left Billy Steel, who wasn't very nice, split the side up because he was very domineering and greedy. He'd arrived as the record ever transfer when McMillan paid £15,500 for him from Greenock Morton. Billy upset a few players with his selfish attitude because he didn't used to bother three games before an international. He used to say: "If I have three good games before an international and then a bad international, I'm a bad player. If I have three bad games before an international and then a good international, I'm a good player." Those were his actual words to me. When he first came to the club, he told me that he'd be away in two years. "That's the only way to make any money in this game," he said. As it turned out, I don't think he made much money in his career because I heard that he finished up bumming it around over in America, after he emigrated there in 1954 and played for a while for the Los Angeles Danes.

When he was at Derby, Steel had a job at Bennett's hardware shop, or at least he was paid to do a job because I don't think he ever went. The shop was owned by the Derby chairman, Ossie Jackson, and it was a bit of a sweetener. Leon Leuty went and asked if a job could be found for him because he was getting on a bit, but they refused him. That resulted in him asking for a transfer and he finished up at Bradford City.

The game against Arsenal attracted the biggest attendance at the Baseball Ground since 1936, so there was a great atmosphere. The journalist covering the match for the Derby Evening Telegraph wrote in his report: 'No team in the country could have stood up to them. The usual immaculate Arsenal machine was thrown right out of gear by the class and speed of the determined Rams.'

We finished fourth that season, nine points behind Champions Arsenal, who ended up seven points clear of Manchester United in second place. I was top scorer that season with 18 goals in all competitions, which was fantastic for a winger. When Raich was there, he fed me balls in behind the full-back and I could get up to have a crack at goal, so I was regularly in double figures for the season. After Raich went and Johnny Morris came in, Johnny used to score them, so then Stuart McMillan asked me to hang out wide and I altered my game.

After finishing third the following season, things deteriorated and we were relegated at the end of the 1952/53 campaign. McMillan was replaced as manager by Jack Barker in the early part of the following season. McMillan didn't have a deep knowledge of football, but he said some things that were pretty intelligent and if you listened, you picked some things up off him.

The people in charge at that time weren't good enough and things got worse under Barker because we dropped down to the Third Division. Barker had been a great player, but he was a poor manager. I don't think he'd updated himself because he still played with an attacking centre-half. Barker had played in the half-back line and they didn't do any pivoting on the centre-half in those days. My dad was the same; he couldn't understand why the full-backs were coming in and pivoting to cover defensively. When I first played for the school team, the wing-halves watched the wingers and the centre-half was in the middle of the field.

I WAS THE LAST member of the Cup-winning side to leave Derby when I left in 1955. I think I was ready to leave when I did. I'd gradually seen the team dismantled and most of the lads who came in were local Derby lads who weren't good enough. I'd been in and out of the side in that last season. I'd lost my son, Michael, at the age of seven and that upset me. When that happens to you, it puts things in perspective and football's not important. We've now got a great grandson called Michael.

My benefit payment was £750 and when income tax was taken off it I received £480. I was due another benefit before they let me go.

Mansfield came in for me, but I went to non-league Boston. We beat Derby 6-1 in the FA Cup in December 1955 at the Baseball Ground in my second season. It is still a record away win by a non-league team against League opponents in the FA Cup. It was Derby's first home defeat of the season and their third heaviest defeat ever in the competition. It was regarded as a totally shock result because they were high up in the Third Division (North) table at the time (they would eventually finish second, just missing out on promotion) and went up the following season, but it wasn't a shock to us! They were slower than us and we were all over them. There were a number of us in the Boston side who had Derby connections. Apart from myself, there was Ray Middleton, who was the manager and goalkeeper, Don and Geoff Hazeldine and Ray Wilkins.

We played Tottenham in the following round and we played wonderfully well, but we couldn't get the ball in the net. Middleton was about 36 by then and very bad on crosses so that's what did us.

I stayed at Boston for a couple of years and then went to Long Eaton as player/coach. I later became player/manager, which was great. I had quite a few of the lads like Norman Nielson and Johnny Poppitt playing for us. They all played for about £4-a-match. I lived in Wilmorton and trained the Wilmorton and Alvaston team at night before becoming player/coach at Alfreton under Jim Bullions. Jim and I have always been good friends and we used to room together at Derby. After Alfreton, I went to Crewton who played in the Central Alliance, which wasn't a bad league to play in. I put a good side together there which included a lot of Derby County 'A' team players and there were also three ex-schoolboy internationals playing for us. Former Derby centre-half Mick Smith came straight from Bradford City to join us and I put him in as a sweeper. I was at Belper Town as a coach after the formation of the leagues in Derby was altered. Whereas Crewton used to get the best amateurs to play in the Central Alliance, others were coming in for them when it all changed. Angus Morrison asked us to go to Belper as their reserve side because they didn't have one.

I finished with two years at Burton Albion with Ken Gutteridge. Ken didn't want any older players, so there were six who were still at school who were playing with us.

Away from football, I was a decorator and worked as a maintenance man at the Co-op when washing machines came out. I spent four years at the County Council and while I was there, I was coaching on Saturday mornings for Derby City Council. They were starting up a programme for kids, running football training after school. I looked after Mickleover and

Ricknald. I built an adventure playground and was the gaffer there. In with that job, we did football coaching and started leagues.

I was working from ten in the morning until eight at night, seven days a week – but we only got paid for 36 hours – and I did that until retirement. I got a civic award for the work I did, which was nice recognition. When people ask me what I got the award for, I say, "Enjoying myself."

I was always involved on Saturdays with different teams, so I didn't get to many Derby games for a while. I went with another former player, Ray Young, to see if we could get some tickets for a match when Cloughie was in charge. "Who are you?" they asked. "I'm not coming again," Ray said as we left empty-handed. 'Youngy' was a schoolboy international who had been at the club for a long time.

I didn't really start going again until Lionel Pickering came in. I was with Jim Bullions and Ray Wilkins at Jack Stamps' funeral and Ray, who knew Lionel because he'd played cricket with him, introduced us to him. Lionel arranged for a couple of tickets to be left on the door for us for a night match. After the game, Lionel said: "There'll be two tickets for you at every home game." He was as good as his word and I've been going ever since. Jim and I are the only ex-players who receive complimentary tickets now because they stopped handing them out this season.

Some of the things the players do today are foreign to me. I look at some of them running all over the field. There are ten men there and when they lose the ball there should be one to pick up apiece, but they don't do it. You see them all running at one player. Nobody said it was going to be easy this season and it hasn't been, but it's nice to see Derby back in the top-flight. Let's hope we can stay there.

JOHNNY MORRIS
INSIDE-FORWARD 1949–1952

BORN   27 September 1923, Radcliffe
SIGNED   March 1949 from Manchester United; £24,500
RAMS CAREER   140 games, 47 goals
HONOURS   FA Cup winners medal: 1948, Division Two
Championship: 1953/54, 1956/57. 3 England caps, 3 goals
LEFT   Transferred to Leicester City, October 1952; £21,500

Johnny cost a British record transfer fee when he was signed from Manchester United. Manager Stuart McMillan paired him with Billy Steel in a bid to find a duo capable of emulating the Carter-Doherty partnership. He made an impressive start to his Derby career, scoring 13 goals in as many appearances to earn an England call-up. A nippy inside-forward with an eye for goal, Morris moved on when it became inevitable that Derby would be relegated in the 1952/53 season.

Derby County 4 v Stoke City 1

League Division One
Saturday 7 May 1949

Baseball Ground
Attendance 28,876

*Morris ends the season with a hat-trick to make it eight goals
in the final three games*

Teams

Stuart McMillan	**Managers**	Bob McGrory
Terry Webster	1	Dennis Herod
Bert Mozley	2	Cyril Watkin
Jack Howe	3	John McCue
Tim Ward	4	Frank Mountford
Leon Leuty	5	Neil Franklin
Walter Musson	6	Johnny Sellars
Reg Harrison	7	Johnny Malkin
Johnny Morris	8	George Mountford
Jack Stamps	9	Syd Peppitt
Billy Steel	10	Bill Caton
Frank Broome	11	Alec Ormston
Morris 16, 31, 38 Harrison 62	**Scorers**	Peppitt 24

Referee: Major F C Green

I TURNED PROFESSIONAL with Manchester United in 1941 after being with Manchester United Junior Athletics Club, otherwise known as Mujacs, since the age of 15. We had a great side and we won the 1948 FA Cup final, which was then known as one of the greatest Cup finals of all time. We beat Blackpool, who had Stanley Matthews in their team, 4-2. It was an excellent team to play in. We had some fantastic players such as Jack Rowley, the centre-forward, and Charlie Mitten, the left-winger, who in 1950 would defect to play in Colombia where there was no maximum wage in an attempt to earn megabucks, and we had an Irish international full-back, Johnny Carey, who captained the Rest of the World side that played against Britain in a post-war game at Hampden Park.

The season after winning the Cup, I was unhappy after losing my place in the side. The line-up used to be announced on the Friday and one week I discovered I wasn't in the team. There was no excuse for leaving me out because we were winning at the time, so I went to see Matt Busby. "What's going on?" I asked him.

"I'm resting you," he replied.

"Well, you can rest me forever then. Put me in for a transfer."

Busby refused my request and furthermore insisted: "While I'm here, you'll never leave this club."

Busby didn't think I'd say anything about being left out of the side, but it doesn't look right in the Press, does it? I was 25 years-old and had to find a way to get away, so I went to see Busby again the following day and told him I was packing football in to become a professional golfer. I was a good golfer at the time, playing off scratch, so he fell for it. People have said that I had a difficult relationship with Busby, but he was my golfing partner and we didn't fall out when I left. In fact, he later asked me: "When are you coming back?"

It wasn't a worrying time for me because I'd been approached by Derby, Liverpool and Leicester, which of course wasn't allowed, but it happened. I had talks at Liverpool with the Moores family who ran the club, but I decided to join Derby, which turned out to be a good move because it was a good club to play for. They looked after the players, shoving an extra two or three quid into your pay packet, whereas

Manchester United were stingy buggers who wouldn't pay the money and Busby looked after himself. I cost the club a record £24,500, which was an unbelievable sum and nearly £10,000 more than the club had paid when setting the post-war record by signing Billy Steel from Greenock Morton. In between England internationals Tommy Lawton [£20,000 from Chelsea to Notts County] and Len Shackleton [£20,500 Newcastle to Sunderland] had upped the figure.

Derby manager Stuart McMillan became my partner at golf, like Busby had been. McMillan wasn't a bad golfer and we played at Keddleston Park. In fact, when he had a word with me about signing for Derby, he picked me up and took me to Keddleston Park. It's a smashing golf course and was one of the reasons why I signed for Derby.

I took Raich Carter's place in the Derby side as he had moved on to become player-manager at Hull City and I had no problem at all settling in. My first goal for Derby was against Manchester City at the Baseball Ground, which was sweet, being an ex-United player. I'd wanted to go to City three or four years before leaving United, but, perhaps understandably, Busby wouldn't let me go there.

McMillan was the nicest manager and it was a joy to play for him in that respect because he was a gentleman, but I don't know where he got his ideas about football from. He wasn't a tactician, so essentially we sorted it out amongst ourselves.

I WENT ON A good scoring run towards the end of the season and ended up with 13 goals in as many games. The match I've chosen for this book came on the last day of the season when I scored a hat-trick in a 4-1 victory over Stoke at the Baseball Ground.

At that time, people were comparing my partnership with Billy Steel to that of the great Raich Carter-Peter Doherty forward line, which had been so successful for Derby. Steel was a busy, 90-minute player, but I rollocked him a few times because he was a bit greedy, hanging onto the ball. I'd let him know what I thought if he'd been selfish. I could have turned him into a brilliant player by stopping him from carrying the ball too far. It was as simple as that. He was an inside-forward, but he'd go back and then carry the ball until he lost it. He wouldn't listen. Beat one man and part with the ball is the secret of football, in my opinion. You see these wingers dancing about on the wing, beating man after man and eventually losing the ball. They want to show off, be the man, but football is a team game about scoring goals and you do that by combining well together. Billy wanted to show everyone how brilliant he was.

My three goals came in a 22-minute spell in the first-half. After I'd opened the scoring, Peppitt equalised for Stoke, but we then dominated the game and Reg Harrison rounded off the scoring in the second-half to complete an emphatic win.

Neil Franklin was in the centre of the Stoke defence. I played with him a few times for the Football League side and he became a big pal of mine. Neil was a good player, but Jack Stamps caused him a few problems that day. I profited because he was frequently drawn out of position when Stamps wandered. Stamps was a big lad who scored a few goals. It was a muddy pitch at the Baseball Ground, so he would get away with things. He never made a goal for anyone else, as he was always shooting at goal, wherever he was.

At the back we had Leon Leuty who was a good centre-half. He played for England and he was in commanding form against the Stoke forwards. Jack Howe at full-back, who also played for England, was another who played very well that day.

Tim Ward was the captain and he was a grand lad. He was the gentleman of football. In fact, I'd say that he was probably too kind to be a footballer because he wasn't domineering at all. I saw him help players by showing him how to do certain things. Tim was quite good at that, but the problem was he couldn't do it himself. Walter Musson, who was a wing-half, was the opposite. He was the hard man of the team.

The match report in the local newspaper referred to 'the amazing Mr Morris playing like two men'. They were going a bit too far there! I did have a good game though, and it's always great to score a hat-trick. We finished the season in third place with Manchester United just edging us out of the runners-up spot.

My 13-goal haul by the end of the season resulted in a call-up to the England squad and I went on a five-week tour of Finland, Belgium, France and Germany. Walter Winterbottom had been a centre-half with Manchester United. Now he was in charge of the team which the selectors picked and that's how he dictated England. I felt he had one or two faults in his lecturing. However the tour went well for me. I played alongside the likes of Stanley Matthews, Tom Finney and Wilf Mannion and scored on my debut against Norway, the fourth goal in a 4-1 win in Oslo. Four days later I kept my place as we came from behind to beat France 3-1 in the Stade de Colombes in Paris. I scored the clinching third goal and thought I'd done enough to retain my position.

Fortunately for once the selectors agreed and I lined up to face the Republic of Ireland at Goodison Park for the first international of the new season. We were expected to win easily, so the selectors chose an inexperienced team giving several players a chance to make thir mark. That meant I was accompanied in the team by my Derby team-mate Bert Mozley, who was making his international debut. It all went wrong however as Ireland won 2-0 thanks to a penalty by Con Martin of Aston Villa in the first half and a late clinching second goal by Peter Farrell. Con was an interesting character. He was a centre-half, but could also double as a goalkeeper and was selected in that position at both club and international level. Apparently that was down to his formative years spent playing the Gaelic game hurling.

In fact Ireland became the first foreign team to win on English soil that day. It's often said that that particular accolade falls to the Hungarians who won so convincingly 6-3 at Wembley in 1953, but actually the southern Irish had beaten us back in 1949. Not that I want anyone to remember that. Several of us paid for that defeat. I was not selected again, and it would turn out to be the only cap that Jesse Pye, the Wolves centre-forward, who had been the star turn of their 1949 FA Cup-winning side, would ever win, while Peter Harris of Portsmouth would have to wait five years for his second and only cap, and that came in a 7-0 thrashing in Hungary. Inside-left Wilf Mannion of Middlesbourgh was dropped for the rest of the season, and Wilf was a wonderful player of fantastic vision and skill. The weird thing was it was all the forwards who took the blame. The entire defence, midfield and goalkeeper, Bert Williams, for whom that was only his second cap, was selected again for the next match against Wales the following month. The likes of Stan Mortensen, Jackie Milburn and Len Shackleton, established internationals, came back in and kept their places after winning 4-1 in Cardiff.

I OPENED A NEWSAGENTS shop in Derby during my time at the club. It was just off London Road, on Grove Street. A pal of mine called Stan Pearson, who used to play with me at Old Trafford and had been the inside-left in the 1948 Cup-winning team, opened a newsagents at Pendlebury and it gave me the idea to open one. I asked the manager if it would be okay for me to open a shop and he gave me the go-ahead. I used to get up at five o'clock in the morning to open up the shop before going to training. I can't see Wayne Rooney doing that!

When I was first at Derby, we didn't have any team-talks, but then we made a poor start to the season and McMillan suddenly decided to have them. I think he decided to do that after I told him that we had them at United, but the thing was he still never said anything himself about how we should play! McMillan was the worst bloke I've ever heard when it comes to talking about football. I've said how much I enjoyed his company, but he hadn't got a clue about the game. He started getting wingers to cut across the pitch with the ball, which was, of course, entirely wrong. When I told him what I thought, he gave up with that particular tactic and we started winning. It sounds as though I'm exaggerating a little, but I'm not.

Things got worse in the 1952/53 season and we started sliding down the table. I could see that things were going wrong, so I decided to leave Derby after three years at the club and ended up joining Leicester City. I still lived in Derby and was all for them avoiding relegation that season, but it wasn't to be. Incidentally, I've got a younger brother called Bill, who also had a spell at Derby, and he still lives in the area.

I won a couple of Division Two titles with Leicester during six years at the club. The manager was called Norman Bullock and I reckon he was the worst manager in the game. Worse than McMillan! He didn't know what he was talking about when it came to football. How he got on, I don't know. He played for Bury for a number of years and was quite a good player. In fact, I knew him when I was younger because I'd caddied for him at my local golf club.

After leaving Leicester, I went to Corby Town as player/manager and had a great time there. They were paying me £15-a-week more than I got for playing in the First Division! The limit was £20 if you were a professional, but because I was now supposedly an amateur they were paying me £35 at Corby and I spent three great years there. I went from Corby to Kettering and then had spells in charge at Oswestry and Great Harwood.

To be honest though, I'd lost interest in football by then. I was a decent golfer and I had to choose between the two sports. You can waste your time at weekends chasing footballers, trying to sign them on or whatever, or you can spend a weekend on the golf course and enjoy it. It's the best game of the lot; you can't beat that game. I played golf for Lancashire and I think I could have made it as a pro. I still play regularly when the weather allows and my handicap now is nine, so I'm still playing to a decent standard. After selling the newsagents in Derby, I returned with my family to Lancashire and got a job selling tyres until retiring.

I don't think football has changed a lot since my day, but they're getting paid more money, I know that. I can't believe what they get paid! There's too much football on TV and you get fed up of watching it. In my view, the secret to enjoying football is to have a bet on the outcome. If you don't have a bet, there's no interest. I don't go to see games very often now. I've probably only been once to Old Trafford in the last 12 months.

In my football career, I think the only mistake I made was leaving at Manchester United because they had a great side. You can't tell the difference in the quality of the football until you play with another team. I don't have any real regrets, however, because I was selected for England when I was at Derby. I can't complain because I've had a good life and really enjoyed it.

BERT MOZLEY
RIGHT-BACK 1945–1954

BORN   23 September 1923, Derby
SIGNED   May 1945 from Shelton United
RAMS CAREER   321 games, 2 goals
HONOURS   3 England caps
LEFT   Retired, December 1954

Bert was a highly talented full-back who worked hard on his fitness, using his pace and quick recovery to good effect. He was unlucky to lose his place in the England team through injury and failed to win an international recall as a member of a Derby side in decline. Bert's career came to a premature end when he decided to start a new life in Canada with his family.

Derby County 6 v Sunderland 5

League Division One
Saturday 16 December 1950

Baseball Ground
Attendance 15,952

Rams edge to victory in 11-goal thriller

Teams

Stuart McMillan	**Managers**	Bill Murray
Harry Brown	1	John Mapson
Bert Mozley	2	Jack Hedley
Jack Parr	3	Arthur Hudgell
Tim Ward	4	Tommy McLain
Ken Oliver	5	Billy Walsh
Chick Musson	6	Arthur Wright
Reg Harrison	7	Tommy Wright
Jack Stamps	8	Harry Kirtley
Jack Lee	9	Trevor Ford
Johnny Morris	10	Dickie Davis
Hugh McLaren	11	Willie Watson
Lee 8,35,67,78	**Scorers**	Davis 29,47
McLaren 27,69		Ford 42,86
		T Wright 72

Referee: A Ellis

I WAS AT NOTTINGHAM Forest as an amateur and played a couple of games for them in the 'A' League. I played for the Rolls-Royce team as well. But it was when I went to Shelton United, who played at the back of a pub, that I was discovered by Derby. I was playing as an inside-forward at that time. Jack Bowers, who was a centre-forward for Derby, came to watch a game and had a word with me afterwards. "You'd be better if you were playing at full-back because of your speed and recovery," he said. Jack taught me how to play at right full-back and things just went from there. The manager of Nottingham Forest played hell with his staff because I slipped through their fingers.

I'd only been to one Derby game as a kid because I was always playing football on a Saturday. I don't know where I got the money from as it was right at the end of the war, but I bunked off school one afternoon and watched the Rams play Arsenal. The next time I went to the Baseball Ground, I was playing for them

I signed as a professional for Derby under Ted Magner just a few months after joining as an amateur. The following year, before the game at home to Preston in November 1946, Jack Nicholas, who had been the right-back since before the war, went down with 'flu, so I was drafted in as his replacement. I never looked back after that.

Stuart McMillan had taken over as manager by then and I didn't really get on that well with him. I think he got the job because he knew the directors. There were about eight locally-born players in the side when I was playing. It's not like nowadays, with all these foreigners playing.

I was noted for my quick recovery. Before we played a game against Liverpool, their left-winger, a quick lad called Billy Liddell, talked to our wing-half Tim Ward. They knew each other after being together in the Army and they were chatting about the players on both sides. 'Who is this young kid you've got at right full-back?' Liddell asked Tim.

"He's not bad, but he's a little slow," Tim replied, having him on.

After the game, Liddell came over to Tim and said: "What do you mean, a little slow? He passed me twice!"

I MADE MY ENGLAND debut against the Republic of Ireland at Goodison Park in September 1949 and conceded a penalty. It wasn't a penalty though and I argued with the referee after he pointed to the spot. "That was a sliding tackle," I told him. "I got the ball before the winger got it."

The England captain, Billy Wright, came over to try and calm me down. "Don't talk like that to the referee because the selectors don't like it," he said. That's how Billy was. He was a goody-goody boy who didn't like anybody arguing. No wonder he won over a hundred caps!

"Bugger the selectors," I replied, "it wasn't a penalty."

After that, I played against Wales and Northern Ireland and was picked to play against Italy. I got injured, however, playing for Derby against Chelsea, when I pulled a thigh muscle after running to try and get the ball. That meant that I had to withdraw from the England team, with Alf Ramsey taking my place, and I never got back in. That was partly due to the fact that Derby dropped down from the First Division to the Third Division in the space of a few years. Tim Ward also said that if I'd have been playing for a London club, I'd have been in the England side and nobody would have got me out of it.

THE MATCH I'VE selected, at home to Sunderland in 1950, was one of the most amazing games I was ever involved in as it produced 11 goals. I can clearly remember how difficult the conditions were on that cold day in mid-December. There was snow on the pitch and the ground was frozen. They wouldn't play in those conditions nowadays.

Jack Lee scored twice to give us a 2-0 lead and then, after Sunderland levelled at 3-3, he went on to score two more goals. To score four goals in a game was a great achievement. Jack, who signed from Leicester, wasn't a bad player at all. Hugh McLaren scored the other two goals for us. Both were from close-range, first with his left foot and then with his right.

We were never behind in the match and much of the credit for the win went to Johnny Morris. Although he failed to score himself, he had a great game. In the Derby Evening Telegraph match report, Morris was said to have: 'wriggled and slithered through the Sunderland defence with a speed that would have put Rudolph The Red-Nosed Reindeer to shame!'

Inside-right Jack Stamps struggled to master the conditions that day, but he was usually an influential player. I've never seen anybody like him for holding the ball up. He was a very fast guy who knew his position. We also had Chick Musson who was a solid defenceman. He played the game hard, did his job and was one of the strongest tacklers I've ever seen. In today's game he'd be sent-off on a regular basis. Reg Harrison was a good right-winger who learned a lot from old England international Sammy Crooks. At the back, Jack Parr was a steady left full-back and then there was Ken Oliver, who we knew as 'Rubber Neck' because he was a very good header of the ball.

Billy Steel had left the club earlier in the season. He was the downfall of Derby County because he cost so much money and just played for himself. The club just dropped after he came down from Scotland. The last time I heard from him he was in Los Angeles and he contacted me via the Chamber of Commerce, asking me if I'd give him a job in Calgary, but I just ignored his communication. He was a slob when he died at the age of 59.

FOOTBALL WAS FUN when I played and we used to have a laugh. The manager would sometimes call a team meeting on a Friday, which the players didn't like. One week, I had the rest of the players on, telling them at the end of training that a meeting had been arranged. "Don't forget about the meeting at 12 o'clock, fellas," I called out before leaving to head off home. They all hung around, waiting for a meeting which never took place. It backfired on me a few weeks later, however, when the manager did actually call a meeting and I was left on my own with him because the others had buggered off home!

I went on an FA tour of Canada in 1950, which ultimately would change my life. George Davis, who'd played for Derby in the early part of the century, lived in Vancouver and he came to see me when we were playing there. Tim Ward and I had dinner with him and he said that we should contact his son Art, who was involved in soccer, when got to Calgary. We got off the train at Jasper where we were met by the Canadian soccer officials who drove us through the mountains to Calgary. Art Davis was there and I travelled with him. We had a splendid time and I loved the country.

Several years later, just before a game at Blackpool, someone called out "Hi Bert" as I ran out onto the pitch with my team-mates. "Now where have I seen that guy before?" I thought to myself as I struggled to put a name to the face. Then it dawned on me that it was Art. He came into the dressing room after the game and we kept in touch after that. We were playing golf in Scotland at one time when he received a telegram informing him that his mother was seriously ill back in Canada and urging him to fly back immediately to see her before she died. Art was a millionaire who owned seven hotels and he'd come over with a brand new Cadillac, which he asked me to put on a boat back to Canada for him. I drove the car to the Baseball Ground and everybody thought I'd had my benefit, but that wouldn't have even bought the wheels!

When George Davis came over and stopped with his family at a place near Nottingham, he told me that Art was going to ask me to go over to Canada to work for him. Sure enough, he did come over and asked me to work for him when we were driving to the ground one day. I was 32 then, so I had started thinking about what I'd do for a job when I finished playing. I spoke to my wife about the offer Art had made. "Jean, I'm going to Canada in January, you can come over in May and I'll meet you," I said. That's all we said about it; we never sat down and talked.

My last game was against Notts County, for whom Leon Leuty was playing, and we were both captains that day. It was a very emotional occasion, especially when all the supporters sang 'Auld Lang Syne' to me after the match finished. That really got to me and it was hard to leave the ground.

I've got very fond memories of playing for Derby, but they screwed me at the end of my time there. With my second benefit coming up, I had a meeting with the directors to tell them that I was calling time on my career and going to Canada. "Oh, great Bert, that's fantastic," they said. "If we take the team to Canada, we'll stop in your hotel."

Afterwards, when it came to talking to the club secretary about my benefit, things turned sour. "Oh no," he said, "you've broken your contract."

"What do you mean, I've broken my contract?" I replied. "I sat down with the directors, explained everything to them and they wished me all the best."

I didn't get my benefit. I could have stopped for another eight weeks, said nothing and collected my benefit and then just walked out, but I went the proper way about it. When I left, they gave me a £100 bonus for ten years' service. So that worked out at the princely sum of £10-a-year!

After emigrating with my wife and children, I ran a hotel for Art, but it didn't work out well at all because it turned out he was the biggest crook in Canada. I left the hotel, had three or four jobs and never looked back. I got a part-time job in a gym, which seemed a natural progression because I've always been into physical fitness. My dad gave me my first weight when I was 14. He worked at a foundry and he brought home a weight they used to weigh the coal with, but I could hardly lift it. Later, when I worked at Rolls-Royce, I used to get up at 6am and run round a field before going to work.

I was lifting weights in my garage when I was playing for Derby. We used to train from 10 am until 12 and then I'd go back in the afternoon to do sit-ups and whatever in the gym. After having my tea, I'd go back in the gym at night. That was my day. I was classed as the fittest player in the country at the age of 27. When I won a competition in London for the best physique and my photograph appeared in a health magazine, I was called into manager Jack Barker's office. "What's all this crap?" he said as he threw the magazine down in front of me. "You've got to stop that because you'll become muscle-bound."

I asked him to explain what he meant by muscle-bound, but he couldn't do it. I explained that I was using light weights to tone the muscles. "If you want me to stop, that's fine Jack, put me on the transfer list right now, because you won't stop me doing it," I said.

"Oh no, don't be like that," he said.

Jack came in as Stuart McMillan's replacement towards the end of my time at Derby and things didn't work out for him because he wasn't really a manager.

I played some soccer in Canada and coached the Western Canada All-Stars to victory over Russia. When they said to me that they wanted to have professional soccer teams in the cities, I told them that they wouldn't because the country was too big. For example, if a team from Vancouver was to play a team in Montreal, they'd have to travel 5,000 miles! Imagine the cost of flying a team out. They're still struggling now to establish soccer over here.

I started doing heavy weights in Canada and for four years running towards the end of the 1950s, I was the weight-lifting champion and Odd Lift champion of Alberta. I also won the 'Mr Physical Fitness', 'Mr Western Canada' and 'Mr Calgary' titles.

I'VE NEVER FORGOTTEN Ted Magner's words when he signed me. "In what other job could you be paid to keep fit?" he said. Even now, at the age of 84, I still work on my fitness, spending an hour in the gym every day. I've owned a gym for 24 years and I take some classes there. They did a TV programme on me in Canada last year, showing my involvement in physical fitness. There's a big place in Victoria who've asked me to go and work for them, but it's too far away.

I got screwed three times in business, but I got through it and I can walk down the street and say 'hello' to anybody because I've screwed nobody at all. Emigrating worked out well for us in the end. We live on the waterfront on Galiano Island, just off Vancouver, which is a beautiful place.

The last time I came back to the UK was when my book, *When Football Was Fun*, came out. I may be back next year because I've got a twin sister, Beryl, and it would be nice to get together on our 85th birthday.

I talk to Reg Harrison every couple of weeks and he helps to keep me in touch with what's happening at Derby. From what I've seen, I don't think they've got the players for the Premier League. I watched them on TV against Tottenham and Liverpool and I think they need some quality players. It's a shame, but I think they'll be back in the Championship next season.

I watch about 130 games a season on TV. There are four games shown every Saturday and we also get Italian games and internationals. The game is played at 100 miles per hour now and every manager in England has the same script. No player can beat a player like we had. I'm talking about players like Stanley Matthews and Tom Finney, who would be superstars nowadays. People go on about David Beckham, but he'd have never made the team in our day because he can't tackle or head the ball. He can bend a ball, but he couldn't have done that in the conditions we faced. The pitches now are like billiard tables and the balls are so light, so they can't go wrong. The balls were so heavy in our day. I took goal-kicks and I couldn't reach the half-way line with them!

I had a good playing career and I think I'd do well in the game today. I played four games in five days when I was in the RAF, so it makes me laugh now when I hear that players are tired after playing one game. It also blows my mind when I hear how much players earn in today's game. It's incredible to think how much they receive for playing football.

KEITH HAVENHAND
INSIDE-FORWARD 1961–1963

BORN   11 September 1937, Dronfield
SIGNED   October 1961 from Chesterfield; £10,000
RAMS CAREER   29 games, 14 goals
LEFT   Transferred to Oxford United, December 1963

Keith made an immediate impact at the Baseball Ground after signing from Derbyshire neighbours Chesterfield, finding the back of the net on a regular basis. However, after suffering a serious knee injury in his first season at the club he failed to make another first-team appearance for Derby. Following spells at Oxford and King's Lynn, Keith was left to ponder what might have been after being forced to quit at the age of 28.

Derby County 4 v Bristol Rovers 1

League Division Two
Saturday 31 March 1962

Baseball Ground
Attendance 8,269

Havenhand stuns Rovers with second hat-trick against them in a season

Teams

	Managers	
Harry Storer		Bert Tann
Reg Matthews	1	Howard Radford
Geoff Barrowcliffe	2	Geoff Bradford
Glyn Davies	3	John Frowen
Ron Webster	4	David Bumpstead
John Moore	5	Joe Davis
Mick Hopkinson	6	Norman Sykes
George Stephenson	7	Harold Jarman
Keith Havenhand	8	Keith Williams
Billy Curry	9	Ray Mabbutt
Jack Parry	10	Ian Hamilton
Don Roby	11	Peter Hooper
Havenhand 1, 41, 49 Stephenson 10	**Scorers**	Hamilton 60

Referee: A Atherton

I WAS BORN IN THE town of Dronfield, between Chesterfield and Sheffield. I played for Chesterfield Boys and we got to the final of the English Schools' Shield. I was always going to be a footballer and I signed for Chesterfield from school as an amateur. There were offers on the table from Sheffield United, Sheffield Wednesday, Bolton and Wolves. I had nobody to guide me at the time really because my dad wasn't pushing me in that direction, so I chose to join Chesterfield because they signed nearly all of the Chesterfield Boys team. I was an apprentice centre lathe turner at a firm in Dronfield while I was playing as a part-timer.

I played and scored for Chesterfield against Manchester United in the 1955/56 Youth Cup final. The likes of Bobby Charlton and Wilf McGuinness were in the United side. In goal for us was a lad called Gordon Banks, who was outstanding. He kept us in it, but eventually we lost 4-3 over the two legs, which was a fabulous performance. I was called-up to the England Under-19 squad and played against Hungary at Sunderland.

After making my debut for Chesterfield at the age of 16, I still played quite often when I was doing my National Service and I signed full-time for Chesterfield when I came out of the forces at the age of 20.

I played nearly 200 games for Chesterfield and scored 60-odd goals. I did well in the 1960/61 season, scoring over 20 times, despite the fact that we got relegated to Division Four. At the beginning of the following season, Derby came in for me. I thought at that time that I'd missed the boat with regards to playing in a higher division. I was linked quite regularly with big clubs in the newspapers and it was reported that Chesterfield turned down a £15,000 bid from Manchester City for me, but nothing happened until Derby made an offer. I think they were just looking for a goalscorer who could make things happen for them in Division Two, after they had spent the time since winning promotion in 1956/57 in the lower reaches of the table, and I happened to be on the doorstep.

It was before the maximum wage was abolished. I was on £15-a-week at Chesterfield and they were only on £20-a-week in the First Division, so there wasn't much of a gap between players in the lower divisions and the top-flight. I was on £20-a-week when I joined Derby and that was all the year round whereas at Chesterfield the money dropped to about £10-a-week in the close-season. That was still fairly good money in those days. I had my biggest pay-day when they did away with the maximum wage, going up to £40-a-week. Johnny Haynes famously became the highest-paid player in the country on £100-a-week.

I made my debut against Liverpool at the Baseball Ground and we won 2-0. I'd signed in the week, went down to the ground on the Friday and then found myself playing the following day. I travelled to the Baseball Ground in my car and didn't really know about the parking arrangements, so I was getting really worried because I was driving round looking for a place to park. I eventually parked in one of the side-streets and set off walking, only getting there about 45 minutes before kick-off. I scored in the return fixture at Anfield at the Kop end, but we lost 4-1. I didn't find the step-up to Division Two to be very difficult because I was loving my football at that time and I soon took to it.

Harry Storer, who had become Derby manager in the close season of 1955 after relegation to the Third Division, was very blunt, but I liked him because you always knew where you stood with him. He took the bull by the horns and told you if you were bad, but he also praised you if you were good. He used to come up to me and say: "You know what I've told you, keep working and when you get a chance to go forward, run at 'em." I was quite skilful and scored a lot of goals with my head, given that I wasn't that tall.

Storer had been a skilful wing-half as a player, good enough to win England caps when he was a Rams player back in the 1920s. As a manager, however, it was all about heart for Storer. Apprently he used to say to the late Tommy Powell as the team boarded the coach for away matches: "How many hearts have I got today, Tom?" And then to emphasise the point, he would then thump his own chest.

Storer was such a character. The passionate manager had an equally fierce-looking dog, Billy, who sat growling outside his master's office, daring any player who wanted to know why he had been dropped from the team to step over Billy and knock on Storer's door. I didn't brave it!

Another tale concerns Sheffield United manager Joe Mercer, who complained to Storer that six Rams players had been over-physical and guilty of clogging in a game between the two sides.

"Give me their names," demanded the Derby manager.

"Why, are you going to fine them?" asked Mercer.

"No, it's the other five buggers I'm after," Storer snapped back.

But despite all that, Harry knew a good player when he saw one. He didn't really subscribe to tactical theorizing. He was more interested in finding out if a play could play.

ONLY A MONTH after joining Derby, I scored the first hat-trick of my career in a 4-1 win at Bristol Rovers. It was the same scoreline in the return game at the Baseball Ground towards the end of the season and I scored a hat-trick that day as well. After doing so well at Eastville, I was looking forward to the home game against them. We were third or fourth in the table at the time and it looked as though a home win was on the cards. I'm sure that during the Bristol Rovers team-talk, the manager would have said something like: "Watch out for him because you know what he did at our place."

I was quite confident of scoring again and so it proved. In fact it was the first minute of the game when I got the opening goal. Mick Hopkinson, who was a wing-half, got to the byline, hit the ball hard and low across goal, which I was anticipating, so I ran across the defender to the near post and got my foot in first to deflect it into the corner of the net.

It wasn't long afterwards when George Stephenson added a second with a firm drive which went in off the woodwork. I scored my second goal when there was a melée in the goalmouth, the ball ran free and I cracked it in. We were 3-0 up at half-time and things were looking great.

When we came out for the second-half, it was on my mind that I might get another hat-trick and it wasn't long before I did manage to score a third goal. When centre-forward Bill Curry broke down the left and crossed it, I was coming in on the inside-right position – with the ball just around the penalty spot – and I got right up and headed it back the way it came. The keeper had no chance as it went straight into the angle. There wasn't a lot of fuss over the fact that I'd scored a hat-trick because nobody used to really celebrate goals in those days. All you really used to get was a hand-shake or a pat on the back and someone would say: "Well done" or whatever. I didn't even get to keep the matchball because that wasn't done at that time!

Rovers pulled a goal back when our goalkeeper Reg Matthews hesitated after coming off his line. Reg was an ex-England international, who had won five caps whilst at Coventry City and who'd signed for Derby at around the same time as me.

The margin of victory could have been greater because I had several other good chances and Curry also missed a couple of openings. Bill Curry was a robust player who'd take the big centre-halves on and knock them out of the way.

As a further indication of our domination, Don Roby and Ron Webster both struck the woodwork. Don joined Derby from Notts County just before I signed. He was a very tricky little winger who stayed on the touchline and I linked up well with him on the right. Like me, he got a nasty injury which finished him. Ron was just a young lad when I was at Derby, but you could see he was going to be a good player.

Jack Parry was the skipper and we all looked up to him. He was from a family of footballers.

In his match report, *Derby Evening Telegraph* reporter Gerald Mortimer commented that I had 'mastered the knack of getting into regular scoring positions'. The newspaper reports on the game were fairly low-key; they didn't go overboard about my hat-trick like they do nowadays.

I'd never scored a hat-trick before joining Derby and then I got two in one season. It was unusual for them to both be against the same team. I think others have scored two hat-tricks against the same team in the same season, but there can't be many who've done it. I don't know what it was about Bristol, but I also used to do well against Bristol City.

A COUPLE OF WEEKS after the Bristol Rovers game, I injured my knee against Norwich and never played again for Derby. There were no subs in those days, so I went back on the field and that made the injury worse. They thought it was a straightforward cartilage problem at first, so I had an operation in Derby Hospital to remove the cartilage and thought that was the end of it.

I joined in with pre-season training but there were problems as soon as I started playing again and it became clear that the injury was more serious than first thought. It turned out that I'd suffered cruciate ligament damage, which was a serious injury. They're able to make replacement ligaments now, but of course that wasn't possible back then.

I tried to get fit and win my place back, but my knee kept letting me down. I played in the Central League, but I kept breaking down. It was an awful time because I'd had a good first season, scoring 14 goals in 26 League games, but I was unable to build on my good start due to the injury.

Knowing that I wasn't going to be able get back to how I had been was hard to accept. Tim Ward had taken over from Harry Storer as manager by the time I left the club. I could have stayed at Derby if I'd wanted to because I had another year on my contract, but there didn't seem to be much scope for me because Alan Durban had been signed as my replacement.

It was terribly disappointing to leave Derby. It wasn't because I wasn't good enough; it was because I couldn't get fit. I was 26 when I left to join Oxford who were in the Third Division. We had a good run in the FA Cup before losing to Blackburn. Ron Atkinson was our skipper and he was a good lad who was a fantastic centre-half. When I left Oxford, Ron moved into my house because it was a club house. I'd got a better house than Ron, so he moved into mine. He always had big ideas, even in those days!

I had a season at King's Lynn, but my knee was giving me problems so I was missing games regularly. When I was 28, a specialist looked at my record and told me that I should pack in playing. I couldn't even play local football, so I've never kicked a ball since. A legacy of my career is that I've had two replacement knees.

When I finished playing, I returned to live in Dronfield and had to look for something to do. I had a friend who was a driving instructor and he asked me if I was interested in driving. I wasn't skilled to do anything else, so I accepted his offer to show me the ropes. I'd sit in the back of his car while he was taking lessons and bought his driving school off him for three or four hundred quid when he became an examiner. When I started my driving school around 1968/69, you didn't have to be qualified to be a driving instructor, so it was easy to get into it. Shortly afterwards you had to be approved by the Ministry, so I sat the relevant exams. When I took the business over, it was one of only two driving schools in the area and I used to work long hours because I was always busy. There are too many driving schools now, but it was a good business to be in back then. I retired 18 months ago after teaching over 2,500 people to drive in 40 years.

I've always retained a strong interest in sport. My lads, Kevin and Andrew, both played for Sheffield Steelers ice hockey team. Andrew was a really good netminder and he played for the Steelers for six years. I'm President of Coal Aston Cricket Club. There's plenty to do there and now I'm retired, I get involved in all sorts of things at the club. I've played cricket all my life and was quite good at it. I never had the chance to turn professional, but I think I could have done if I'd stuck at it.

I'm interested to see what Derby are doing. I received an invitation to go to the first game at Pride Park and I think it's a lovely stadium, but I've not been for a couple of years. I do look back and think what about what I might have achieved in the game had it not been for the injury which ruined my career. I'd played all my football in the lower divisions before suddenly being given a chance to play at a higher level, which I snapped up, but I only had three quarters of a season in the Second Division before it was snatched away from me.

DAVE MACKAY
WING-HALF 1968–1971

BORN 14 November 1934, Edinburgh

SIGNED July 1968 from Tottenham; £5,000

RAMS CAREER 145 games, 7 goals

HONOURS 22 Scotland caps, First Division Championship: 1960/61, Second Division Championship: 1968/69, FA Cup: 1961, 1962, 1967, Scottish League Championship: 1957/58, Scottish Cup: 1956, Scottish League Cup: 1955, 1959, First Division Championship (as manager): 1974/75

LEFT Transferred to Swindon Town, May 1971; £30,000

Dave enjoyed much success both sides of the border, helping both Hearts and Spurs win an array of honours, before linking up with Derby at the age of 33. Brian Clough's decision to play him in a sweeper role proved to be a master-stroke, giving him a new lease of life as he helped Derby win the Second Division title in his first season. Dave later returned to the club as Clough's successor and guided the Rams to further glory in winning their second League title.

Derby County 5 v Tottenham Hotspur 0

League Division One
Saturday 20 September 1969

Baseball Ground
Attendance 41,826

Two new club records set as MacKay leads Rams to a famous victory over his former team

Teams

Brian Clough	**Managers**	Bill Nicholson
Les Green	1	Pat Jennings
Ron Webster	2	Phil Beal
John Robson	3	Cyril Knowles
Alan Durban	4	Alan Mullery
(sub. Frank Wignall)		
Roy McFarland	5	Mike England
Dave MacKay	6	Peter Collins
John McGovern	7	Jimmy Pearce
Willie Carlin	8	Jimmy Greaves
John O'Hare	9	Alan Gilzean
Kevin Hector	10	John Pratt
Alan Hinton	11	Roger Morgan
		(sub. Tony Want)

Durban 15, 70, Hector 19, **Scorers**
Carlin 23, O'Hare 62

Referee: L Callaghan

AT THE AGE OF 33 in the summer of 1968, I was all set to leave Tottenham and go back to Hearts as player/manager, but I didn't really want to go back there to play because I'd put on so much weight and I was getting a bit slow. Hearts had always been my club and after all the great times I'd had there, I didn't want people saying: "Oh, look at that wee fat guy there!" So when Brian Clough phoned up and offered me the chance to join Derby, it provided me with a get-out.

I don't know how Brian found out that I was going back to Hearts, but he came down to London to tell me about his plans. With his neat suit, collar and tie and hair in a quiff, he looked more like a trainee bank manager than a football manager. He spoke in glowing terms about players like Roy McFarland ("I picked him up from Tranmere for peanuts and he'll be England's next centre-half"), John O'Hare ("a brilliant player") and Kevin Hector ("the finest goalscorer in the Football League"). Brian went through the team, giving a description of each player. From the way he was talking, you'd have thought they were all superstars!

The conversation then turned to me. "I want you to be the captain and play as a sweeper, controlling it all from there," said Brian. I'd never played as a sweeper before because I was always up and down as a midfield player, but the idea appealed to me. I thought that the role would allow me to carry on playing for a few more years. Despite the fact that Derby had finished fifth from the bottom the previous season, Brian was adamant that they were on the verge of big things. "If you come to Derby, we'll win the Second Division," he said. When you sat and listened to Brian, you believed what he was saying because his enthusiasm was infectious. And what he predicted came true of course because we walked the Second Division. I decided there and then that I wanted to join Derby.

That first season at Derby, 1968/69, was the easiest season I had in my whole career. The thing that changed everything for me was the new position. With the likes of Roy McFarland, Colin Todd and Archie Gemmill racing about and making tackles, I was left to just patrol at the back, picking up the pieces and passing the ball, which suited me down to the ground. I joke to people that I could still be playing now if that was my role.

There were some really great players at the club. We went to Norwich in the penultimate game of the season and won 4-1 to clinch the title. Brian's persuasion also meant that I was the joint winner of the Footballer of the Year award, alongside Manchester City captain Tony Book. I'd been so close to winning the award on a number of occasions in previous seasons at Spurs, so I was delighted with the accolade.

IN THE EARLY PART of the following season, our first back up in the First Division, came the match I've chosen to highlight. We'd made a good start to the campaign and were unbeaten in our first ten games before facing Tottenham at the Baseball Ground. We had a chance to set a new club record of 22 League games without defeat, stretching back to March. Spurs boasted the best away record in Division One and had won their previous four away games so we knew it wasn't a foregone conclusion. In fact it would be a very difficult game.

There were some new faces in the Spurs line-up, but I knew the majority of them very well from my time at White Hart Lane. Jimmy Greaves wasted no time in making a comment, running over to me on the pitch and, with a smile on his face, saying: "Didn't think we'd be seeing you this quickly."

The ground was packed – setting a new attendance record at the Baseball Ground, which was never broken – and the fans were treated to an impressive performance as we swept Spurs aside. We were 3-0 up after 25 minutes.

With a quarter of an hour gone, Alan Durban opened the scoring when he took advantage of some uncertainty in the Spurs defence, nipping in as centre-half Mike England hesitated, and then slipping the ball past Pat Jennings. Alan and Willie Carlin were tough, industrious midfielders. Kevin Hector increased our lead just a few minutes later, receiving the ball from John O'Hare and holding off Peter Collins before firing home. Kevin was a natural goalscorer who reminded me of Jimmy Greaves. He was something special, getting goals out of nothing.

It was 3-0 midway through the first-half when little Carlin got his head on the end of a corner from Alan Hinton when England and Collins both failed to clear. O'Hare made it 4-0 just after the hour-mark with a super goal. Carlin and Durban combined superbly with the latter laying the ball off to O'Hare who smashed it past Jennings. O'Hare was probably an under-rated player to some people, but not to me. He was a great centre-forward because he was as strong as anything and held the ball up well. He was a good passer as well. That made him a really great front-man. Durban completed the scoring, heading in a cross from Hector who did well to keep the ball in when it looked to be going out.

I was amazed at how good we were. We'd just come up from the Second Division and were now amongst the big boys, but we still put on a great show. It was a fantastic to win by such a big margin, but I did feel a bit sorry for Tottenham after the game because I'd had a great time there. Put it this way, I'd have rather beaten Arsenal 5-0! I'd had so many good times at Tottenham and they were my favourite English club but you have to work hard and do what you can for your own club. And on that particular day, Derby were so much better than Tottenham.

I felt embarrassed for my old manager, Bill Nicholson, who was a gentleman as always, shaking my hand after the game. Talking to journalists afterwards, Bill called us "a very, very wonderful team" and went on to say: "They humiliated us. They are very talented and they don't just run, they know when to run and where." He then paid me a handsome tribute, saying: "If I wanted all this to happen for anybody it would be him. Six Dave Mackays and you wouldn't need anybody else. He's an inspiration to everybody and a credit to the game. I rate him as one of the all-time greats." That was typical of him because he was a generous man. He'd wanted me to go back to Hearts instead of joining Derby. Johnny Harvey was the Hearts manager at the time and he'd met Bill in the forces. Some years later, when I was manager of Derby, we beat Spurs 8-2. No wonder Bill Nick didn't want me to join Derby!

GOALSCORERS GRAB THE headlines, but we shouldn't overlook the players whose job it was to stop goals going in at the other end. Les Green, for example, made a world-class save from Greavesie early in the game. The ball look destined for the roof of the net when Greavesie caught it on the volley, but Les dived and caught it. If it had been from anyone else, I'd have expected him to have made the save, but coming from Greavesie, who was so close in, made it extra special. It wasn't just the fact that he made the save, he also caught the ball. Greavesie looked astonished when Les made the save. I'd say it was the best save I've ever seen and that includes Gordon Banks' famous effort to keep out Pelé's header in Mexico. That could have changed the game if the ball had gone in.

Greavesie was always a threat and Roy McFarland and I had to make some important tackles to stop him going through. Roy Mac was superb that day. We had some very good defenders but I think McFarland was the best defender at the club. He was consistent as well. The full-backs, Ron

Webster and John Robson, also did well. They didn't come more solid than those two.

The win over Spurs saw us set a new club record, but then we lost the following week at Sheffield Wednesday. We suffered a mid-season slump, losing too many matches to mount a serious challenge for the title. That was a shame because we finished the season strongly, winning eight out of the last ten games and drawing the other two, ending in fourth place.

I was ever-present the following season – the only time I achieved that in my career – as we finished in ninth place. As I was coming towards the end of my playing career, I decided that I wanted to give management a go to see what would happen. Swindon came in with an offer for me to go there as a player with a view to becoming player/manager. Although it wasn't a fantastic offer, I decided to go there. I soon found that it wasn't as easy as it had been at Derby and Tottenham. When Fred Ford resigned as manager the following November, I was named player/manager.

A YEAR AFTER TAKING charge at Swindon, Nottingham Forest came in for me. As Forest are Derby's big rivals, I don't think I was very popular in either camp! I spent 11 months at Forest before being given the chance to rejoin Derby. I was watching the reserves at Northampton and I saw the Derby chairman, Sam Longson, after the match. I thought straight away that something was happening because I knew he hadn't come to watch those two teams. He told me that he wanted me to come back to Derby to replace Brian Clough who'd walked out of the club. I was reasonably popular with the players after being at the club previously and Sam said that I was the only man in the country who could replace Clough. He wanted someone who could unite the players, board and fans at such a turbulent time. I'd had such a good time at Derby previously, so I readily agreed to go back.

It was a tough start because the players hadn't wanted to lose Clough and his assistant, Peter Taylor. After the success Derby had enjoyed under Clough and Taylor, everyone wanted them to stay. If I'd still been at the club as a player, I'd have been one of the first ones to try and stir things up. I'd have done my damnedest to try and keep Clough and Taylor there. I would have even had a chat with them to try and persuade them to stay. The fans were on Brian's side as well because he'd been so successful, making Derby one of the best teams in the country.

Knowing most of the players so well, I knew who I'd be most popular with. And I knew there were certain players who wanted to join Clough again, so I let them go. I had to win the League title because I knew that when I achieved that, it would put me on a level with Clough and Taylor who'd only won it once.

I signed Franny Lee first and foremost because he was a real man who wouldn't stand for any bickering behind the scenes. If Franny heard anyone complaining about things I'd asked them to do, he'd say: "He's the manager and you've got to play for him." I fancied him as a player as well, of course, but I thought his character and experience were vital ingredients.

We won the title in my first full season in charge, which was fantastic. If you've won the First Division title just once in your career, you've done brilliantly. You'd like to do it every year, but sometimes it's just not possible.

As WE PREPARED for the start of the 1975/76 season, I managed to sign Charlie George who went on to become a great hero at the club. I was in Scotland when my assistant, Des Anderson, told me that Charlie was for sale. If you'd asked me at that time who I wanted to bring to the club, I'd have picked out Charlie. But I'd have thought there was no way of taking him away from Arsenal. I phoned Arsenal straight away and they confirmed he was available. Charlie was close to joining Tottenham at that time, but I spoke to him and he told me that he wanted to come to Derby. He turned out to be a great signing because he brought something extra-special to the front-line.

We finished fourth in the 1975/76 season and then, after a disappointing start to the following campaign, I left the club. There was a story in one of the newspapers suggesting that I was going to leave, so I went into the boardroom and had an argument with the directors. I don't know who was behind the story, but I decided it was time to go. "I've had enough here, so I'm moving on," I told the directors. Without naming names, I didn't really like one or two members of the board. After Clough's departure, the club was in something of a crisis because some were supporting Clough and others were supporting me. It was the same in the boardroom. I left knowing that I'd done a good job at the club.

I had a spell at Walsall before managing in Kuwait, which was the best time I had abroad. In eight years there, I won the Championship five times and the Gulf Cup. I earned plenty of money over there as well. I came back to England to manage Doncaster Rovers and then Birmingham City. Doncaster didn't have a particularly good team at that time and there was no money to spend on strengthening it. When you go down to that sort of level, it's very, very difficult. Birmingham was another hard job.

I went abroad again in 1991, going to Egypt to coach Zamalek, which is a club near Cairo.

A couple of years later, I was appointed as the national youth coach of Qatar. I was in charge of the Under-18s and we went to Uruguay for the Junior World Cup. That was great because just to qualify for the tournament was a feat. I remained in Qatar until 1996, taking my time in the Middle East to around 13 years in total.

Every time I went abroad, my family remained in the East Midlands. We bought a house in Burton Joyce when I was at Forest – which is about four or five miles from the ground – and it's still our family home.

Nowadays I attend all of Derby's home games. I go in the Brian Clough Lounge and have a meal before sitting out in front of the restaurant to watch the game. It's a nice day out and I enjoy it. My autobiography, *The Real Mackay*, was published by Mainstream Publishing in 2004. I enjoyed looking back on my career and recalling so many wonderful moments.

I make regular trips back to Scotland to see family and friends. Unfortunately, the last time I went up there, I saw my Hearts team lose 1-0 in the Edinburgh derby against Hibs. My wife is a Hibs supporter and that's why I don't talk to her!

STEVE POWELL
DEFENDER/MIDFIELDER 1972-1985

BORN 20 September 1955, Derby
SIGNED   November 1972 from Apprentice
RAMS CAREER   408 games, 21 goals
HONOURS Division One Championship 1974/75, 1 England U23 cap
LEFT   Retired 1985

As a schoolboy prodigy Steve had his pick of clubs before opting to sign for Derby, the team his father Tommy had starred for. He was equally at home in defence or midfield and became Derby's youngest-ever player when he made his debut at 16 years and 30 days old. Steve was tipped to go on and win full England honours, but injuries took their toll and prevented him from realising his early promise, forcing him to quit at the age of 28.

Derby County 1 v Liverpool 0

League Division One
Monday 1 May 1972

Baseball Ground
Attendance 39,159

Rams finish the season with vital win over close challengers for the title – a victory which, following an anxious wait, sealed Derby's first Championship

Teams

	Managers	
Brian Clough	**Managers**	Bill Shankly
Colin Boulton	1	Ray Clemence
Steve Powell	2	Chris Lawler
John Robson	3	Alec Lindsay
Alan Durban	4	Tommy Smith
Roy McFarland	5	Larry Lloyd
Colin Todd	6	Emlyn Hughes
John McGovern	7	Kevin Keegan
Archie Gemmill	8	Brian Hall
John O'Hare	9	Steve Heighway
		(Sub. John McLaughlin)
Kevin Hector	10	John Toshack
Alan Hinton	11	Ian Callaghan
McGovern 62	**Scorer**	

Referee: C Thomas

I PLAYED FOR TWO YEARS running with England Schoolboys, which was quite unusual. That came about because I played a year ahead of my age the first season. A number of my team-mates went on to make the grade in the game, including striker Ray Hankin, left-back Kevin Beattie, goalkeeper Barry Siddall and midfielder David Price.

I could have gone to most clubs at that time, but Derby suited me because it was my home-town club, so I signed schoolboy forms and then became an apprentice. My father Tommy had made over 400 appearances for Derby as an inside-forward from the war to the early 1960s, so I suppose it was a natural progression when I joined the Rams. I don't actually remember my father playing, but I followed Derby as a kid.

I was 15 when I left school and I'd just turned 16 when I got in the first-team. I held the record for being Derby's youngest player until Lee Holmes took the record recently. Age didn't come into it because if the gaffer thought you were good enough, he'd play you. At one time, managers wouldn't play players until they'd had a fair amount of experience on the ground staff, but that wasn't the case at Derby under Cloughie.

My debut was in the Texaco Cup against Stoke on a Wednesday night and the following Saturday, I was a substitute against Arsenal and came on for the last half an hour. I played a full game the following week against Forest, but then I didn't play again until the Liverpool game at the end of the season.

IT'S AMAZING TO THINK that the Liverpool match was only my second full appearance. Ron Webster, who normally played at right-back, got injured the previous week against Manchester City, so I filled in for him. When the team was first announced, I think there were a few fans wondering whether Cloughie had made the right decision or not. With both teams battling it out at the top of the table, it was obviously a very important game. But when you're young, you just want to play, so I probably didn't realise the true importance of it. I had plenty of confidence in my own ability and I honestly didn't feel nervous. I just went out and enjoyed it. I wasn't really given any specific instructions before the game. I was just told to go out and play my own game. The way we played was very simple anyway.

I was fortunate that I was in a side full of good players who were performing at the highest level. It's a lot easier to go into a side like that rather than one that's struggling. Top players can play their own game and help others as well. Others have it all on just to play their own game.

With so much at stake for both clubs, it was understandably a very tense affair. I was up against Steve Heighway and the Liverpool side also included the likes of Emlyn Hughes, Kevin Keegan and Ray Clemence who all went on to play many times for England.

There weren't many real goalscoring opportunities in the first-half. Perhaps the best chance fell to Kevin Hector who forced a good save out of Clemence. If there was anyone you wanted the ball to fall to in the penalty area it was Kevin because his goalscoring record was phenomenal.

In the second-half, goalkeeper Colin Boulton sent Keegan to the ground as his momentum carried him through and Liverpool manager Bill Shankly later claimed they should have been awarded a penalty. Liverpool then created their one real clear chance of the game when Keegan beat Todd and laid the ball invitingly across the box, but it was beyond both John Toshack and Boulton.

Just a few minutes later, John McGovern scored what proved to be the only goal of the game. Hector's throw-in found Archie Gemmill whose lay-off was dummied into the path of John McGovern on the edge of the penalty area, he swung at the ball as he was falling over and it went in. McGovern was a very under-rated player who did a fantastic job wherever he went.

Liverpool put us under pressure after that, as you'd expect, with substitute John McLaughlin testing Boulton with a shot which he did well to push away. Colin was a tremendous keeper with great hands who could have been a professional cricketer.

Despite having to weather some pressure, it wasn't all about defending as Hector and John O'Hare caused problems for the Liverpool defence. O'Hare was a tremendous centre-forward. You knew if the ball went up there that nine times out of ten it would stick, which was fantastic when you were defending.

Roy McFarland dominated against Toshack and Todd also had an excellent game. I would say that Roy was the best all-round player I was ever associated with. For a centre-half, he had a fantastic amount of skill. Unfortunately, he didn't win anywhere near the amount of England caps he should have done, mainly due to injuries, which was a shame because he was a tremendous player.

There was much relief when the game was over and we'd secured two points. I was satisfied with my performance and Gerald Mortimer, writing in the *Derby Evening Telegraph*, commented: 'Powell was brilliant. Not brilliant for a 16 year-old: just brilliant. Other players gave him the ball with confidence and he did not let them down. Such is his skill that anyone can pick him out now as a future England player.'

We faced an anxious wait because we'd completed our fixtures while Liverpool and Leeds both had a chance to pip us to the title on the last day of the season. That wouldn't happen now, of course, because they play all the final fixtures on the same day. The first-team squad travelled to Majorca, waiting for the outcome of the matches involving Liverpool and Leeds. As I was still an apprentice, I was left back in Derby, cleaning boots while the senior players were living it up in Majorca.

We didn't expect the results to go for us because Leeds looked likely to get at least a draw at Wolves who weren't a top team and Liverpool were quite capable of going to Arsenal and winning. As it turned out, Arsenal drew and Leeds lost, handing us the title. Some people say we won it by default, but at the end of the day, it's how many points you get over 42 games, isn't it? It doesn't really matter when you get them.

For a club like Derby to come through and win it was unheard of really, particularly as there were some powerful teams like Liverpool, Leeds and Arsenal around. Unfortunately, I didn't make enough appearances to earn a championship-winners medal.

As WELL AS WINNING the First Division title, we also won the Texaco Cup and the Central League that season. I was a regular in the Central League that season, so I got a medal. Winning the Central League title was some achievement itself because Liverpool totally dominated it for years. The reserve set-up was different then because the teams were made up of players who weren't in the first-team or players who were maybe on the transfer list, so there were some good players turning out in the Central League. Now it's more of a mix of youth players. We played Liverpool in the Central League one Friday night and there were 10,000 people at the Baseball Ground! We opened one year against Manchester United and the attendance was about 8,000. Manchester United's side was so strong they could probably have played in the old Second Division.

It was a fantastic time to be in football in general and certainly at Derby. From being a mid-table Second Division club, within two years we were playing the likes of Real Madrid and Benfica in the European Cup, which was amazing. I played in the semi-finals against Juventus, which was a fantastic experience. We lost 3-1 over there and were held 0-0 back at Derby. We missed a penalty and if that had gone in, we'd have had 15-20 minutes to put them under some real pressure. We were more than capable of beating them at home by the required amount and when we didn't, it was very disappointing. I know they play a lot of games now in the Champions League, but I think the European Cup was a better system. You can win the Champions League now having not won a domestic title, which doesn't seem right.

WE PUT UP A disappointing performance in the league the season after winning the title. I had a couple of runs in the side, playing in either defence or midfield. I was just happy to play, to be honest, so I wasn't really fussed where I played. Early on in my career, I felt I was more suited to playing in midfield, but when injuries started to take their toll, I wasn't mobile enough to play in midfield, so I saw myself more as a central defender playing off a centre-half.

Brian Clough was a really difficult act to follow when he left in 1973, but Dave MacKay did a fantastic job. He steered us to the title in the 1974/75 season and I played in just enough games to win a medal. In the following season, we were going well until Charlie George dislocated his shoulder against Stoke. We had a couple of big league games coming up and then had Manchester United in the semi-finals of the FA Cup. After losing to United, everything just went downhill and that was the start of the demise. Before the semi-final, we were in with a chance of doing the 'double'. But then we lost a couple of league games and drifted down the table.

Colin Murphy was the reserve-team coach and he stepped up to take charge following Mackay's departure in 1976. I appeared as a guest player for a South African team called Arcadia Shepherds in 1977. I was due to spend six weeks out there but I dislocated my shoulder at the end of the first week, so I had to come back to England the following week.

Tommy Docherty was named as Derby's new manager in the early part of the 1977/78 season. One player who wasn't happy when Docherty came in was Gerry Daly. He'd left Manchester United because he didn't get on with Docherty, so the last thing Gerry wanted was for him to take over at the Baseball Ground.

I got on okay with Docherty, but he never really spoke about the game with much authority, like Brian Clough and Peter Taylor did. He did a lot of things on the spur of the moment and seemed to get by on reputation rather than being a good manager. You've got to have some sort of stability at a club to be successful, but that didn't happen while Docherty was there because there were so many players coming in and going out and that was how he tended to manage. He didn't have great success as a manager, when you actually look at his record, yet he always seemed to land jobs.

I personally did well in the 1978/79 season, missing only one league game and winning the Player of the Year award, but it was a difficult time as we finished just a place above the relegation zone. Docherty got rid of players like Charlie George and Colin Todd that season. If you get rid of quality players, to maintain the standard you've got to replace them with players of similar quality and I don't think he did that. When that happens, the standard goes down and that's what happened.

IN THE SUMMER OF 1979, I went to America, where I played for Tulsa Roughnecks. They just took over my contract so I was getting the same money that I got at Derby. Alan Hinton was the coach and Roger Davies, David Nish and Colin Boulton were also out there. The Americans really gave it a go to try and get the game off the ground, throwing a lot of money at it to bring in some world stars, but they had no foundation to build on. The big-name stars like Pele and Franz Beckenbauer made an absolute fortune in America, but Tulsa just took over my contract so I was on the same money that I received at Derby. I had a fantastic time out there and we did quite well, getting through to the Conference final against New York Cosmos. We beat them at home and then lost at their place in front of a 70,000 crowd. I enjoyed my time out there because it was a great experience.

Back home, Colin Addison replaced Docherty as manager and I didn't meet him until I returned from America. I missed the first month of the season because I was still in America. It was an unusual situation to be in because I played continuously for 21 months, which was stupid, but we didn't really think about it. I ended up getting an injury due to wear and tear. A lot of the pitches in America were Astroturf and I ended up with pelvic inflammation due to over-playing on hard surfaces.

We were relegated at the end of the 1979/80 season and things went steadily worse after that, resulting in Addison being replaced by John Newman in January 1982. I snapped the cruciate ligament in my knee the following month and that was the beginning of the end for me as far as my career was concerned. We were playing at Leicester and I went up for a header with Alan Young, who was a big striker. As I came down, I landed half on his foot, half on mine and felt something snap in my knee. It was painful but I got up and walked off. My knee then swelled up so I went to see a specialist a week or so later after the swelling had gone down.

I thought I'd just done a cartilage because that was the standard type of injury you suffered, but the specialist examined the knee and told me that I'd totally ruptured the cruciate ligament. He explained that carbon fibres could be put in the knee, but they have no natural elasticity so they're either too tight, preventing the knee from bending fully, or they don't offer enough support. They replace it with a natural ligament now to get the natural elasticity.

The club surgeon told me that he didn't recommend the operation, advising me instead to keep my quads strong. About four or five years later, they began successfully performing surgery on cruciate ligament problems. I was out for about six months and I played for a couple of seasons after that but I was never right and I started getting more problems. I wasn't as mobile and there would be swelling after games, which wouldn't go down for three or four days, so it would be difficult to train some weeks. At that level, you can't get by without training because you've got to keep that level of fitness up.

THERE WAS ANOTHER CHANGE of manager towards the latter end of 1982 when Peter Taylor came in. It was said that Brian Clough was unhappy when Taylor signed John Robertson without having spoken to him, but I don't really know what the true story was. It was sad really that they fell out because life's too short for things like that to happen.

Mike Watterson had taken over as chairman and there were a lot of things happening behind the scenes at that time. When we were relegated to Division Three at the end of the 1983/84 season, Taylor had been replaced by McFarland towards the end of the campaign and then Arthur Cox took over in the summer.

I was continuing to experience problems with my knee and the game against Reading in April 1985 proved to be my last appearance. I came off and my knee was swollen again. I went for another operation where the cartilage was taken out, but that failed to work as I was told the problem was due to wear and tear. I went down to London to see a specialist called Nigel Harris and he told me it was time to finish playing. It was really disappointing, but when you play a contact sport, there's always that chance that you'll get an injury which will seriously harm your career or finish you. When I retired at the age of 28, I'd had 12 years in the game, but it would have been nice if I'd had three or four more years because Derby enjoyed success under Arthur Cox during that time.

It would also have been great to have won a full England cap after playing at Under-23 level, but if you're not good enough, for whatever reason, you don't get picked. It's difficult to say whether things would have been different if I hadn't been troubled by injuries because it depends on the quality of players around at the time.

After sorting out my insurance pay-out, I went to Shepshed as a coach and ended up becoming player/manager. From there I went to America as head coach of a team called Albany Capitals before returning to Shepshed as a player under Martin O'Neill who was very shrewd. A lot of people have tried to imitate Cloughie's style and have failed in many cases, but he had a lot of similar traits and he's had a fantastic career in management. I had another spell as manager of Shepshed following Martin's departure before spending about 18 months as manager of Burton Albion.

I then managed Belper for a season before being offered a full-time post at Mackworth Tertiary College in 1991. It's now part of Derby College and I manage the fitness centre at the Prince Charles Avenue campus. The college has first call on the facilities in the daytime and the Council take it over in the evenings and at weekends, taking bookings like a normal Council-run leisure centre. I've always been interested in the leisure industry and it's been fantastic because I've really enjoyed working there. It's a great atmosphere to be in and I meet lots of different people all the time. We try and help people to get fitter and lose weight or whatever and when you succeed in doing that, which we regularly do, it's really pleasing.

I only live about ten minutes away in Kirk Langley, so I can actually walk to work in about half an hour.

I've not seen much of Derby for a couple of years. I went for a while when they got into the Premier League for the first time but football doesn't have the same appeal now, to be honest, because money totally dictates the game. Sky dictate when matches are played and it's not a working man's game anymore. If you take a couple of your kids to a game it probably works out at more than £100, which is a helluva lot of money for an afternoon out.

When I look back on my career, I had some great times so I've got some fantastic memories, particularly from the early 1970s.

ROGER DAVIES
STRIKER 1971-1976 & 1979-1980

BORN   25 October 1950, Wolverhampton

SIGNED   *1:* September 1971 from Worcester City; £12,000. *2:* September 1979
from Tulsa Roughnecks

RAMS CAREER   157 games, 43 goals

HONOURS   First Division Championship 1974/75

LEFT   *1:* Transferred to Brugge, July 1976; £135,000. *2:* Transferred to Seattle
Sounders, March 1980

Roger was a tall, gangly forward who was good on the ball for a player of his
size. After being plucked out of non-league football, he played in the Derby
reserves and had a spell out on loan before making a massive impact in his
second season at the Baseball Ground. Roger forged a highly effective strike-
partnership with Kevin Hector and featured prominently in Dave Mackay's
1974/75 title-winning side.

JIM BULLIONS — 1946
DERBY COUNTY 4 v CHARLTON ATHLETIC 1

Nearing a Cup final means all sorts of interest in you and we were asked to pose for this photo before our match at Coventry the weekend before we took on Birmingham in the semi-final at Hillsborough. That's me on the back row, second from left between trainer Dave Willis and Jack Parr.

It was a wonderful day out at Wembley for all Derby fans, who packed the old open terraces and gave us fantastic support.

Skipper Jack Nicholas receives the 1946 FA Cup from King George VI.

Our victorious Cup-winning side take the lap of honour.. As the
youngest member of the side it was a dream come true for me.

My 1946 FA Cup-winning buddies: Back row left to right: Parr, Bullions, Nicholas, Woodley, Howe, Leuty, Musson. Front row left to right: Crooks, Stamps, McMillan (manager), Doherty, Carter, D. Willis (trainger). On floor left to right: Harrison, Duncan.

(Left) The plate we were given by the club to mark our victory.

(Right) I still have my medal and it means everything to me.

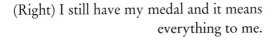

I loved my time on the right wing at Derby and as a lad learned a lot from pre-war international Sammy Crooks, who sadly missed out on a place in the Cup-winning team..

It was fantastic to play with the brilliant Raich Carter and Peter Doherty too. In this photo of the Derby frontline you can see me on the left, then Carter, Dave McCulloch, Doherty and Dally Duncan.

This photograph shows me scoring the fourth goal against Blackburn Rovers during our 5-0 win in December 1947. I scored 59 goals in 218 official games for the Rams, although I also played during the war, but the games and goals in that period don't count in official statistics.

We had a very good team spirit, although an afternoon singing songs was more common than a night on the tiles! Here Billy Steel and Raich Carter tinkle the ivories on the Palace Theatre, Grimsby's organ with the legendary organist Reginald Dixon (white jacket) lending a helping hand.

The Rams team which played Manchester United in the 1948 FA Cup semi-final. Back row: Stuart McMillan (maanger), Tim Ward, Bert Mozley, Leon Leuty, Jock Wallace, Jack Howe, Chick Musson. Front row: Me, Raich Carter, Jack Stamps, Billy Steel and Angus Morrison.

Here I challenge the Manchester United defence. Sadly we lost 3-1.

Some may say the goal I scored to defeat that fantastic Arsenal team was a bit lucky, but I will maintain that I meant to shin the ball from Allen Oliver's cross past Walley Barnes on the line.

Here I am today with some mementoes of my career.

For a few years Derby was a great place to play football and I was proud to captain the side. That's me on the right, shaking hands with Middlesbrough's Wilf Mannion.

The team that began the 1949/50 season after rounding the previous season off with a great 4-1 victory over Stoke in which I scored a hat-trick.

I was proud to play in a fantastic Derby side.

Then and now: I won the first of my three England caps on tour in Norway in May 1949, scoring the first of my three goals.

At home with some of my memories of a fabulous career at Derby.

The incredible game against Sunderland had 11 goals and every kind
of excitement you could possibly imagine.

Relaxing on an away trip with my team-mates. That's me with the pipe at the back of the group.

The early 1950s weren't the best era for Derby, but we had some good players in the team. In this group you can see: (Back row, left to right): Oliver, Myself, Middleton, Barrowcliffe, Bell, McLachlan. (Front row, Harrison, Morris, Stamps, Parry and McLaren)

Playing at the packed Baseball Ground was a great experience. In this picture we are playing Spurs in 1952, a game we drew 0-0.

Chelsea centre-forward Roy Bentley takes a ride on my back during an FA Cup replay at Stamford Bridge in January 1953.

It's great to relive the memories of my career, which was sadly ended by injury after just one season in the Derby first team.

My team-mates from 1963. Back row: Barrowcliffe, Swallow, Waller, Oxford, Young, Matthews, Curry, Ferguson. Front row: Myself, Hutchinson, Cullen, Parry, McCann, Durban.

My hat-tricks against Bristol Rovers are a rarity; two against the same opposition in the same season, home and away.

DAVE MACKAY — 1969
DERBY COUNTY 5 v TOTTENHAM HOTSPUR 0

When Brian Clough persuaded me to come to Derby he said we would win the Second Division. he was right and this was the team which did it.

Celebrating one of the five goals we scored against my old club Spurs as we announced our return to the top flight.

Alan Gilzean goes close for Spurs in that game.

We always had some great battles against Tottenham and I enjoyed
marking my old mate Jimmmy Greaves (left).

Derby fans have always been wonderful to me.

Captaining Derby back into the top flight and then helping to lay the foundations for the first title success was fantastic towards the end of my playing career.

Signing for Derby as a callow teenager. In attendance are my father, Tommy (back left), who himself played over 400 games for the Rams and the incomparable Brian Clough.

I made over 400 appearances during my Derby career, but that first title victory was incredible because I was so young and we won it in such a strange way.

Liverpool goalkeeper Ray Clemence punches clear from Roy McFarland during the game which ultimately won us the title, with Emlyn Hughes in attendance.

Here Roy McFarland outjumps Chris Lawler, who is climbing all over me
to get airborne.

Clemence saves from Kevin Hector, but John McGovern scored the vital
goal and we won 1-0.

The 1971/72 Championship-winning side show off their medals.

Posing with the manager Brian Clough (right) and the captain Dave Mackay (at rear) after making my debut as a 16-year-old.

Winning the League title was an unbelievable experience. Here l lift the trophy along with Colin Boulton as we parade around the packed Baseball Ground

Kevin Hector and Ron Webster showing off our haul of trophies to a young Rams fan in 1971/72.

The Cup replay at Tottenham has gone down in Rams history as one of
the most remarkable ever. To have been a part of it and scored a hat-trick
as we came back to win 5-3 was fantastic.

Getting in a shot at White Hart Lane despite the attentions of Spurs' Welsh international central defender Mike England.

Scoring one of my 43 goals for Derby.

PETER DANIEL – 1974
ATLETICO MADRID 2 v DERBY COUNTY 2

Playing in European competition has to be at the top of any player's career highlights and our incredible tie against Ateltico Madrid was certainly the most amazing match I played in during my 15 years at Derby.

Winning the 1974/75 League title was an incredible experience
and it was great to see such celebrations again so soon after our
first championship triumph.

Success brings many things, including a civic reception at the Town Hall.

I may have been a squad player for much of my Derby career, but I loved every minute of it and when Roy McFarland's injury gave me the opportunity to play throughout most of 1974/75, when we won the League title again and had that fantastic tussle with Atletico Madrid in the UEFA Cup, I jumped at the chance.

I scored goals wherever I went in football, but starting out at Derby and bagging the four in the game I have chosen against Hartlepool was something very special for me.

Having a laugh with Derby County legend Jack Stamps.

The Derby squad in 1984. Back row, McFarland, Livingstone, Blades, Palmer, Hindmarch, Steele, Pratley, Garner, Clifford, Buckley, Guthrie Front row: Devine, Hooks, Taylor, Davison, Burns, Cox, Powell, Myself, Robertson, Harbey, Irvine

I had a great time as manager at Northampton Town, winning promotion from League Two in my first season, 1999/2000.

I love being still involved with the game as manager at non-league Corby Town.

I scored 31 goals in 144 games for Derby, but none were more important than the goal against Sheffield United that virtually sealed promotion to the top flight at the end of the 1986/87 season.

Getting a header in towards the West Brom goal in the run in to the season, which ultimately saw us promoted.

Taking on the Tranmere defence single-handed.

Celebrating after the final home game of the season against Plymouth,
which we won 4-2 to clinch the Division Two title.

Arthur Cox was a fantastic manager for both me and Derby County.
Winning promotion was the pinnacle of his time at the Baseball Ground.

Moving to Derby after having a terrible time in London playing for
Palace gave me a new lease of life and I loved every minute of it.

My trademark goal celebration came out to show everyone what it meant to score against my old club Sunderland in such a vital game.

Tangling with Sunderland's Dariusz Kubicki.

Promotion is another goal nearer thanks to Dean Sturridge's strike.

Celebrating with Deano at the final whistle of the last home game of the
season against Crystal Palace which brought us those vital three points to
clinch promotion.

I scored 60 goals in 210 games for Derby,
a record of which I am very proud.

Ian Taylor opened the scoring very early on against Forest with this tremendous shot from just inside the box.

I had a tremendous tussle with Forest's David Johnson after he came on as an early substitute.

Everyone piles in to celebrate Pesch's remarkable goal. The Kenco coffee cup which defeated Forest keeper Barry Roche is on display in the Derby trophy room, signed by Pesch!

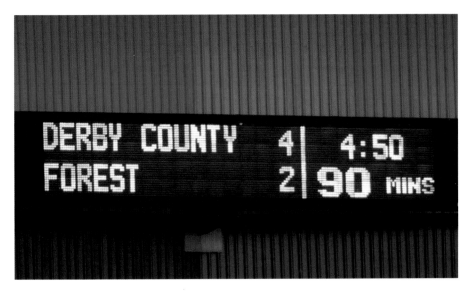

I realise that seeing a scoreboard like this is a delight for Derby fans, and it meant something special to me to beat my boyhood team in such a vital relegation battle too.

Saluting the fans at the end of a well-deserved victory.

Playing for Derby has been
a great experience, and captaining the team
to promotion in 2007 was something I will never forget.

Stephen Pearson's first goal for Derby couldn't have come at a more important place or time - Wembley Stadium in the play-off final...

...much to the delight of all Rams fans.

Pearson and Jon Macken rejoice at the final whistle after we had clinched promotion in a tense game. It was a magnificent moment, but I had to feel sympathy for my old team-mates.

Returning to Pride Park with the trophy and to hordes
of happy Rams fans was fantastic.

There is nothing better than winning at Wembley. Especially at the new Stadium, which had only been opened a few weeks before.

Club captain Michael Johnson (left) and captain for the day Matt Oakley show off the Play-off final trophy back at Pride Park.

Tottenham Hotspur 3 v Derby County 5

FA Cup fourth round replay
Wednesday 7 February 1973

White Hart Lane
Attendance 52,376

Davies hits hat-trick as Rams produce a stunning comeback

Teams

Brian Clough	**Managers**	Bill Nicholson
Pat Jennings	1	Colin Boulton
Ray Evans	2	Ron Webster
Cyril Knowles	3	David Nish
John Pratt	4	Terry Hennessey
		(sub. Alan Durban)
Mike England	5	Roy McFarland
Phil Beal	6	Colin Todd
Alan Gilzean	7	John McGovern
Steve Perryman	8	Archie Gemmill
Martin Chivers	9	Roger Davies
Martin Peters	10	Kevin Hector
Ralph Coates	11	John O'Hare
(Sub. Jimmy Pearce)		
Chivers 20, Gilzean 44, England 78	**Scorers**	Davies 80, 86, 107 Hector 68, 113

Referee: D Biddle

I WAS AT WOLVES AS A kid, which I didn't really enjoy, then Walsall picked me up for a while, but nothing came of that. I did my apprenticeship in engineering but all I ever wanted to do was play football.

I played for Bridgnorth and then Worcester City, where I scored seven goals in my first three games and suddenly the national newspapers were linking me with all the top clubs in the country.

Derby were one the clubs and Peter Taylor came to take a look at me when I was playing in a game at Barnet. I scored two goals in the first-half and Peter left at left-time. As he was leaving, he saw a scout from another club in the car park, who asked him about me. Peter told him he was wasting his time and said to not bother looking at me. I signed for Derby shortly afterwards! The fee of £12,000 was a record for a non-league player.

I got a phone call telling me to go to Derby, so I went there and met Brian Clough for the first time. He was a legend even then, so I was over-awed when I met him. It was the same when I played in the reserves at Everton shortly afterwards in a midweek game. It was my first time playing at a big ground and I remember thinking how great it was to be introduced to players like Alan Durban and Terry Hennessey. I'd been watching them on television only a few weeks before and suddenly there I was playing with them. It was a like a dream that had come true for someone like me who'd come out of non-league football. It was only in later years that I really appreciated how lucky I was to make a career out of playing football because there were lots of lads who came out of non-league football, played for about a year professionally and then went back to where they came from. Luckily for me, I did have a career out of it.

I have a lot to thank Cloughie for. He formed a great double act with Taylor and you won't get anyone like them in the game again. It was a real 'good cop, bad cop' routine.

In my first season at the club, we won the Championship and the reserves won the Central League, so it was a great time.

I ACTUALLY MADE MY League debut during a spell on loan at Preston under Alan Ball snr, but I didn't really enjoy it there. I told Cloughie how

I felt and asked him if I could come back and play in the reserves. He was very understanding and agreed to take me back straight away.

My League debut for Derby came at Manchester United in November 1972 – playing up front alongside Barry Butlin – and we got a roasting that day, losing 4-0. I scored my first League goal three weeks later in a 5-0 win at home to Arsenal as we looked to defend the League title, but we would eventually finish in seventh position. I had a good run in the side and scored a few goals, including the winner against Peterborough in the third round of the FA Cup. That set up a meeting with Tottenham at the Baseball Ground in the next round. We didn't play well that day and had to settle for a replay after a 1-1 draw. I scored with a toe-poke past Pat Jennings after the ball fell to me about six yards out following a free-kick from Colin Todd.

THE FIRST GAME HAD been forgettable, but the replay turned out to be a classic as we came back from 3-1 down with 12 minutes to go to win 5-3 in extra-time. We played some great stuff in the first-half and didn't deserve to be 2-0 down at half-time. Things just went Tottenham's way.

Martin Chivers opened the scoring after meeting a cross from Cyril Knowles. It looked for all the world as if it wasn't going to be our day in the first half. We put Tottenham under pressure with Terry Hennessey just failing to get on the end of a good cross from Kevin Hector and John McGovern shooting narrowly wide after Hector had back-heeled to him. Then I forced a save from Pat Jennings after beating Phil Beal to the ball. Hector hit the bar and an effort from Archie Gemmill struck Alan Gilzean on the line, which was unbelievable, before Tottenham increased their lead a minute before the break. After a throw-in on the right, the ball was crossed to Gilzean who headed in at the second attempt after his first effort came back off the bar. It was an injustice that we were behind at half-time because we'd played so well.

The second-half was only a couple of minutes old when Spurs threatened to score a third and we had Colin Boulton to thank for making a brave save at the feet of Chivers. We now felt that things were starting to go our way and the relentless pressure we put Spurs under paid off midway through the half when Hector pulled a goal back with a hooked shot. It seemed only a matter of when and not if we'd equalise, but Spurs seemed to make the game safe when they scored again to make it 3-1. That goal should never have happened. They were awarded a free-kick when Ron Webster was penalised for hand-ball after being pushed in the back by Ralph Coates and falling onto the ball. When the free-kick was driven in, John O'Hare was ruled to have handled the ball and the referee pointed to the spot.

It was a dubious penalty and John, who is one of the nicest men I know, pushed the referee as he argued about it. He was lucky not to get sent-off. Mike England converted the penalty to put Spurs 3-1 up with 12 minutes to go. The home fans thought that was it, game over, and they were singing: "Wembley, Wembley."

But we refused to throw in the towel. Within two minutes, I took advantage of some uncertain defending, firing through a packed goalmouth to make it 3-2. Then I equalised six minutes later with an effort which won me the Goal of the Month award. There was a throw-in and O'Hare told me to get in some space, which I did, and when John crossed to me from the byline, I flicked the ball up and volleyed it in. I was mobbed by my team-mates as we celebrated the goal. We'd totally deserved to be level in the game and now felt as though we could go on and win.

Hector went close to scoring a goal which surely would now be a winner, testing Jennings with a shot. When the ball rebounded to him, we had a good shout for a penalty when he appeared to be fouled, but the referee was having none of it.

With the match tied at 3-3, it went into extra-time. We continued to dominate in the first period of extra-time without finding the net. Then, just two minutes into the second period, I completed my hat-trick to put us ahead for the first time in the match. Hector sent over a corner from the right and I was there at the far post to head beyond Jennings and the defenders on the line. We were all over them and it was 5-3 six minutes later when Hector got on the end of a long-ball and beat Beal for pace before slotting past the advancing Jennings.

It was a great performance from us because we murdered them. George Edwards, writing in the *Derby Evening Telegraph*, described it as a display "which must rank among the best by any Derby side at any time". He added that it was "the day that Derby showed London how and why they won the championship". Commenting on my contribution, Edwards said that I had become "one of football's big names". That meant a lot to me.

I've still got the signed match-ball as a memento of the hat-trick. The three goals took my tally to seven in five games and I was getting a lot of coverage in the Press. Reporters from all the nationals wanted to talk to me about my hat-trick, but Cloughie told me not talk to any of them. A journalist from one of the tabloids called at my home and said he wanted to interview me. "I'm not allowed to because Mr Clough told me not to talk to anyone," I told him. He assured me that everything would be fine. "It's okay because I'll write the story and then ring Mr Clough and clear it with him," he explained. I was young and quite naive, so I agreed to do the interview. When the piece appeared in the paper the following morning, Cloughie gave me a roasting because the journalist never spoke to him, as he'd promised! I had to apologise to Cloughie. He was going to fine me before deciding to let me off.

We fancied our chances of going all the way in the FA Cup and we beat QPR 4-2 in the following round. I scored to keep up my run of scoring in every round and Hector hit a hat-trick. Kevin was very unfortunate to win only two caps for England. He was a very under-valued player. People don't realise how good he was. For me, he's the top man at Derby. Fans called him 'The King' and he always will be. Kevin still plays for the ex-Rams, but he doesn't have a lot to do with the club itself. The fans would love to see him, but we can't get him to do anything, which is a great shame.

Our FA Cup hopes were ended when we lost to Leeds in the quarter-finals. Having won the League the season before we were also playing in the European Cup and we reached the semi-finals when I was sent-off against Juventus in the second leg. It was out of pure frustration. I was supposed to have head-butted their player, but I actually missed him and he made a meal of it. I'd missed out on playing in the goalless first leg in Italy due to a groin injury, so I sat there on the bench watching the Juventus players cheating, kicking our players and getting them booked. The whole game was just a farce and it was very frustrating just sitting there and watching it. I was fit enough to play in the return match and the Juventus players got up to their tricks in that game as well. They'd wind you up, not only kicking you, but blocking you and tugging your shirt. It happened time after time and when we missed a penalty, I think that just pushed me over the top. I'd already given the defender who was marking me a good whack in the first-half and when he blocked me again, I tried to head-butt him and off I went. If we'd have scored the penalty, I might not have reacted like that. We lost 3-1, but at least Juventus lost the final to the fantastic Ajax side of Johan Cruyff, who collected their third successive European Cup.

I ended up with 13 goals in 25 appearances, which was a good return in my first season. I was a bit of an enigma. I wasn't the archetypical big, lanky centre-forward because I wasn't that physical for my size. I could see a pass that was difficult and I know I had good control for a big guy. Whenever I see the Sky Sports commentator Martin Tyler, he calls me 'The White Kanu'. People often commented that I found easy things hard and hard things easy. I liked to entertain and do things off-the-cuff. I played with a smile on my face because I enjoyed playing and still do.

I learned a lot from John O'Hare about how to hold the ball up. I'd taken John's place in the forward line, but Cloughie still included him in the side, switching him to midfield because he'd got a good footballing brain.

WHEN IT CAME TO picking out a memorable match I played in, it was a close call because I scored five goals against Luton during the 1974/75 season when we won the title under Dave Mackay. Everything I touched that day went in. It was frightening to think how many goals I could have ended up with that day. The keeper made about three saves and I even had two disallowed, so I could have scored seven quite easily! It was one of those games players have in their career. I've got the ball from that game as well. The match was during a hard Easter when we played three games in four days. It didn't bother us, though. When they moan now about playing a few games in a fortnight, it's unbelievable.

Apart from Kevin Hector and myself, the likes of Bruce Rioch and Franny Lee were also regular scorers that season, so the goals were spread throughout the team. With that team, we were always going to score goals. If the opposition scored two, we'd score three. Mackay liked to entertain and see goals. He was a bit like Cloughie in the way that he never worried about the opposition. The way he saw it, if we did our own thing, the goals would come and we'd win the game. Dave was a joy to play for. I did extra work in training with Des Anderson at that time, which I used to enjoy.

AFTER THAT GLORY, my career didn't progress as I would have liked. I did my cartilage on the pre-season tour of Scotland and missed out on my one and only chance to play at Wembley in the Charity Shield. That was one of my biggest disappointments. Charlie George, who played in my place against West Ham, gave me his shield, which was nice of him. When I was sold to Belgian club Brugge in the summer of 1976, I was sad to leave because I loved the club and still do. I didn't get off the best of starts at Brugge, but things turned around and I ended up having a fabulous season. We did the 'double' and I scored 20-odd goals and won the Player of the Year award. The fans loved me at Brugge and I enjoyed it very much.

I returned to England to join Leicester in December 1977. I was Leicester's record-signing at that point, but the move proved to be an absolute nightmare. I'd injured my spine in the Belgian Cup Final, which caused me problems. I joined a struggling side and my first game was against Derby, which we drew. I put in a good performance in the following game, but things went downhill after that and it was an absolute nightmare. I don't know why it didn't work out. I enjoyed being at the club, but I'll probably go down as one of the worst players in the history of the club. When you're a club's record-signing, with all the expectations that go with that and it doesn't work out, it's embarrassing, to be quite honest. I felt sorry for the Leicester people. Somebody said to me that it was like putting a spoonful of hot water into a bucket of cold; it wasn't going to change everything. It was the one spell in my career I'd rather forget.

Jock Wallace came in as manager and he was great with me. After letting me go to America, he came over to see me play in a game when I'd been named the MVP (most valuable player). "Why didn't you play like that for me?" he asked me afterwards, with a smile on his face.

I had a great time in the States. I'd always wanted to go there and I got a chance to play football there after signing for Tulsa Roughnecks. I went out with Alan Hinton and we also had former Derby colleagues David Nish and Jeff Bourne with us in the team. Steve Powell came out for a summer and there was Don O'Riordan as well. When Alan moved on to Seattle Sounders, he took quite a few of us with him including 'Nishy', 'Bourney' and Bruce Rioch. We also had the likes of Steve Daley, Tommy Hutchison and Alan Hudson, so we had a really good side. We had three great years in Seattle and I really enjoyed it. The intentions are great with regard to football in America, but it will never take off there because they can't compete with the other sports.

I came back to Derby in 1979, but it wasn't the same and it didn't work out. I later played for non-league Gresley Rovers when David Nish was the manager before taking over as player-manager myself when he left. I carried on playing in local football for years, which I thoroughly enjoyed.

I'M STILL VERY MUCH involved with Derby. For a start, I now run the ex-Rams team and we play in charity games. Players who regularly turn out include Kevin Hector, Trevor Hebberd, Paul Williams, Andy Garner, Dick Pratley, Phil Gee and Craig Ramage, so we've got quite a good side. We enjoy seeing each other and of course playing football.

I also act as a co-commentator on Derby games for Ram FM, which I enjoy, as well as doing some match-day hospitality work at Derby and organising the forums, which are really good fun. We get the likes of Roy McFarland and Dave Mackay coming along to reminisce about the old days. My day job is at Rolls-Royce as a value engineer. All the lads I work with are Derby fans, so we have some great banter.

That night at White Hart Lane regularly crops up in conversation when I talk to supporters. People seem to associate me with that game. I still get fans coming up to me telling me they were there. Just a couple of weeks ago, a guy came up to me at a match and told me that his mum and dad went to the Tottenham game on their first date! It's great to hear things like that.

PETER DANIEL
DEFENDER 1964–1979

BORN   22 December 1946, Ripley
SIGNED   December 1964 from apprentice
RAMS CAREER   231 games, 7 goals
HONOURS   First Division Championship winners medal 1974/75
LEFT   Transferred to Vancouver Whitecaps, February 1979

Peter gave loyal service to Derby, spending over 14 years at the club. A steady
defender who featured either at centre-back or left-back, he was a bit-part player
for the majority of that time. But when an injury forced Roy McFarland to miss
virtually all of the 1974/75 season, Peter did a superb job as his deputy, helping
the Rams win the League title and in a fantastic European adventure.

Atletico Madrid 2 v Derby County 2
(4-4 on agg; Derby won 7-6 in a penalty shootout)

UEFA Cup, second round, second leg
Thursday 6 November 1974

Estadio Vicente Calderon
Attendance 35,000

Rams knock-out Spaniards after two fantastic games and a tense penalty shoot-out

Teams

Juan Carlos Lorenzo	**Managers**	Dave Mackay
Miguel Reina	1	Colin Boulton
Gonzalez Capon	2	Ron Webster
Panadero Diaz	3	David Nish
Rodriguez Adelardo	4	Bruce Rioch
(Sub. Perez Marcelino)		
Jiminez Benegas	5	Peter Daniel
Villario Eusebio	6	Steve Powell
Fernandez Alberto	7	Henry Newton
(Sub. Ignacio Salcedo)		
Suarez Luis	8	Archie Gemmill
Jose Garate	9	Roger Davies
Javier Irureta	10	Kevin Hector
Ruben Ayala	11	Franny Lee
Luis 4, 82	**Scorers**	Rioch 54, Davies 64

Referee: F Biwersl

I WAS A LOCAL lad and was spotted when I played for Stanley Common in a five-a-side tournament which featured all the local sides in Derby and we got to the semi-finals. I was invited for a trial at Derby and then they asked me to join as an apprentice. Tim Ward was the manager back in 1964. After about 18 months, I signed as a professional when I was 18. I'd followed Derby's results as a kid but I'd never actually been to a match, so it was incredible for me.

I held down a regular first-team place in the 1965/66 season, but I was only a bit-part player during the following eight seasons. I played when required and was quite good at standing in for players, either at left-back or in central defence. I always thought that I could have been a regular in another team, but I enjoyed myself at Derby so I never pressed for a move. I had talks with Luton during Cloughie's time in charge, but that came to nothing. I also played in a practice match for Sheffield Wednesday but again, nothing materialised there. They were the only two clubs who were interested that I knew of, although, of course, players were often left in the dark over such matters back in those days. It wasn't like today where agents are touting their players for a move.

WHEN WE WON THE League title in the 1971/72 season, I captained the reserves to the Central League title in the same season. Even though I didn't make a first-team appearance that season, I went away to Majorca with the senior squad while the title-race was decided. Cloughie was very forthright. He knew what he wanted and he let everybody know what he wanted. If you didn't shape up, you were out. I survived because I was there all the time he was there, so I must have been doing something right.

My big chance came following Cloughie's departure when Roy McFarland ruptured his Achilles tendon playing for England and I was called on to take his place in the side at the start of the 1974/75 season. It was initially thought that he'd be out of action for about half the season, but his recovery wasn't as swift as they expected, so I ended up playing virtually all season.

I myself was injured and I was on pain-killers most of the time because I tore a muscle in my pelvic bone at the beginning of the campaign, so I hardly did any training because of that. I'd play a game, then come in and have treatment, do a little bit of training and then play again.

The first game of the season was at Everton. We drew 0-0, but played well and we felt afterwards that we had a possibility of doing something. Dave MacKay's philosophy was that he wanted us to go forward because he wanted to see goals. If we let a couple in, we were quite capable of scoring three or four. That meant they were good games to watch.

Because we had finished third the season before we had qualified for the UEFA Cup. We beat Swiss side Servette Geneva 6-2 on aggregate in the first round and I scored a rare goal in the first leg 4-1 win. That set up a meeting with Atletico Madrid, who had been beaten the previous May in the European Cup final by Bayern Munich although only after a replay. The first leg was played at the Baseball Ground. It was a fantastic night and a great game, but the Spaniards were the favourites to go through to the third round after scoring two valuable away goals in a 2-2 draw.

We won 1-0 at Leeds in the League before flying out to Spain, which was a great result. Rotation policies were unheard of in those days, so Dave MacKay named an unchanged side to face Atletico. We got off to a bad start when we went behind after only four minutes. The German referee penalised Archie Gemmill for a foul on Ayala and Adelardo's free-kick was met by Luis, who beat Colin Boulton with a free header. Some good chances went begging as we failed to draw level by the break. Franny Lee nearly found a way through after being set-up by Gemmill and Bruce Rioch fired over from a good position following a cross from David Nish.

The gaffer had insisted before the match that Atletico were vulnerable at the back and we proved that in the first-half, without being able to exploit their weaknesses. It wasn't all one-way traffic though because Atletico were playing well and their impressive passing was causing problems for us. Alberto had an effort which skimmed the top of the bar and also put another shot over.

A challenge from Ron Webster on Garate in the area sparked penalty appeals which were dismissed by the referee. Ayala shot wide early in the second-half and then I had a chance at the other end, forcing their goalkeeper Reina, who is the father of the current Liverpool keeper Pepe, to save with his legs.

But we got back into the game when we equalised in the 54th minute when Roger Davies got his head to a cross from Kevin Hector and Bruce Rioch applied the finish. The Kevin Hector then put us ahead ten minutes later, chesting the ball down before firing home after a cross from Gemmill. The Spanish supporters voiced their displeasure, calling for manager Juan Carlos Lorenzo to be axed. Lorenzo had been in charge of the Argentinian national squad at the 1966 World Cup which had been branded 'animals' by Alf Ramsey after their brutal quarter-final match against England at Wembley.

On this occasion Luis saved his bacon, making the scores level at 2-2 on the night. Henry Newton was ruled to have handled the ball and Luis bent the resulting free-kick beyond Boulton. Henry, who was just known as 'H', was my room-mate. Like me, he later had a Post Office for a few years after finishing playing.

Moments earlier, Newton had gone close to scoring after linking up well with Lee. We had a scare when Garate failed to punish a mistake from Steve Powell and Boulton then made a great save at the feet of the same player. Other than that slip-up, Powell was superb. Gemmill also deserves a mention for his performance as he ran non-stop. It was his 200th game for Derby and was surely one of his best displays. Archie always kept working and you wondered where he got all his energy from.

With the match tied at 4-4 on aggregate, we went into extra-time which came and went with no further addition to the scoring. That meant a penalty shoot-out was required to settle it. It was 2-2 on penalties after Rioch and Hector scored for us and Boulton failed to keep out efforts from Luis and Ayala. The pendulum swung in Atletico's favour when Davies saw his spot-kick saved by Reina and Salcedo tucked away his penalty.

Nish found the back of the net to keep our hopes alive and we were given another boost when Capon fired over. Lee and Irueta scored to make it 4-4 and take it to sudden death. Gemmill, Newton and Powell all held their nerve to score while Benegas and Garate found the target for the hosts. The tension was mounting at this point, especially for Ron Webster and myself. There had been the five nominated penalty-takers and then it had gone to six, seven and eight, so now there was only me and Ron left in the centre-circle. You don't think it's going to go that far and we weren't sure which one of us was going to go up first. When it's not really your job to score goals and you are waiting and waiting as the competition goes on it is very nerve-wracking. Thankfully, it didn't come to that because Boulton dived to his right and turned Eusebio's penalty against a post, saving us the problem. I was delighted and relieved simultaneously!

Atletico were very noble in defeat .Their manager, Juan Carlos Lorenzo, hugged Archie Gemmill outside the dressing rooms shouting "Magnifico", a fitting tribute to two hours of quality and stamina from the Derby captain that secured our place in the third round, but we failed to make further progress in the competition. We beat Velez Mostar 3-1 in the first leg before losing 4-1 in Yugoslavia to go out 5-4 on aggregate.

IT WAS A DIFFERENT story in the League, however, as we went from strength to strength. We were winning regularly and we knew we had a good chance of winning the title just three years after Brian Clough master-minded Derby's first-ever Championship success. As we got towards the end of the season, there were more and more superstitions. Players wanted to be in the same position in the line-up as the previous week when we ran out onto the pitch, so as not to upset things. My superstition was to run out second to last. One or two players would wear the same clothes. It's funny how things like that develop when you play football.

When Roy Mac got fit towards the end of the season, people thought he'd been recalled just because he was available again. However, the truth was I could hardly walk by then because the pain was so bad, so he regained fitness just in time really. I don't know whether Mackay would have let me finish the season in the side when returned to full fitness if I'd been fit, but there was no choice because I just wasn't able to carry on. He'd have prob-ably still picked Roy because he was the best centre-half in the country at the time.

Towards the end of the season, there was a poll for the best centre-halves in England and I came fifth in that. I also won Derby's Player of the Year award and we went for a meal at a local nightclub to celebrate. Ipswich, who were playing Manchester City that night, had a chance to pip us to the title, but they only drew and the result which made us champions was given out just as we were about to eat. There were people jumping up and down on tables and we never did get to eat our food.

It was a magical time for Derby. Everybody in the team mixed well; there were no cliques at all, so it was a wonderful atmosphere. Everybody would fight for everybody else. If an opposition player picked a fight with one of our players, we all piled in. We felt that the other side had to do something special to beat us.

Colin Boulton was a good keeper. He was my Best Man when I got married but I've not seen him for years. My central defensive partner, Colin Todd, was very quick and we had a good understanding. We decided right from the off that I would attack everything – making a tackle or heading the ball – and he'd pick all the pieces up. It worked really well. I committed myself and if the ball was flicked past me, Colin was there to sweep up.

At full-back we had Ron Webster and David Nish. I never saw Ron in my first year at the club because he had quite a lot of injury problems at the start of his career. David was one of those players who made it look silky smooth and easy. It wasn't fair because he made everything look ridiculously simple.

I WAS STILL HAVING problems when we came back for pre-season training ahead of the 1975/76 campaign. I tried to get fit for the Charity Shield match against West Ham at Wembley, but I wasn't ready at all. I was included in the party at Wembley, though, because MacKay wanted me to be part of it. Everyone who played in the match was handed a medal and Franny Lee gave me his because he'd already got two or three. Not many people know that he gave me his medal. It was very kind of him and I really appreciated the gesture. You had to do something really bad to fall out with Franny, ask Norman Hunter! They famously had a fight on the pitch during a game and were both sent-off. I didn't play in that particular match because I was injured, so I had a clear view of them still fighting when they were in the tunnel.

I was told that if my injury didn't clear up after two or three months, I'd have to have an operation to put it right. Fortunately, the complete rest I had sorted it out and the muscle started to knit back onto the bone, so surgery wasn't required, but it took me until the end of the season to recover completely.

I was a little frustrated at not being able to build on the success I had enjoyed in the previous season. It would have been interesting to have seen what would have happened if I hadn't suffered the pelvic injury. I don't know whether I would have kept my place in the side. It was some consolation that I was being kept out by Roy Mac, who was the best player in the country in my position.

I can't complain about the way I was treated because I found Mackay to be very fair. There were some who didn't like him, but I found him to be fair. When they accepted his resignation, it was ridiculous because we were still doing well.

BEFORE TOMMY DOCHERTY'S first game in charge, he made me feel ten foot tall. For whatever reason, he announced in front of everybody that I was going to be in the team before naming the rest of the side, which really made me feel good. He didn't play me a lot, but he was quite good to me and eventually gave me a free transfer to Vancouver Whitecaps. When I came back to England from Vancouver, he rang me at home to thank me for what I'd done for him. If you're prepared to work hard for a manager, they appreciate it. The way I looked at it was that all I could do was to do my best every time and I always gave my best for Derby County. Docherty was manager of QPR by then and I think he may have been planning to ask me whether I wanted to play for him there. But before he even had a chance to ask me, I told him that I'd finished with football by then. He said that he just wanted to thank me for what I'd done for him.

My wife Shirley and I enjoyed it in Vancouver and in some respects we wished that we'd stayed there. I signed for two years, but we didn't go back for the second year because we both had our parents in England and we were a bit home-sick. We now realise that we'd have had a nice life if we'd stayed over there. They worked hard and played hard over there. The people said that if you worked hard, you got your rewards for it.

The football in North America was quite good really. I was coming towards the end of my career and there were a lot of players in a similar situation. We had Alan Ball with us at Vancouver, along with my long-standing Derby team-mate Kevin Hector. Another former Derby player at Vancouver was Alan Hinton, who was the assistant-manager there when I first went. He knew he was getting someone who'd work hard for the team and not just go out there and have a nice time.

When we played in New York, it was the only time I've been frightened playing football. We had Scottish international Willie Johnstone on the left wing and he was beating the full-back all the time. The guy was getting totally frustrated. Every time Willie put the ball past him, he was brought down. He kept his cool for a while but then he just lost it and had a fight with the full-back. A New York player, who was rumoured to have been linked to the Mafia, ran to join in so I had to go and help Willie. It took the referee about five minutes to sort it out and he sent-off both Willie and the full-back, along with the other Cosmos player involved. It all calmed down, but then our goalkeeper, Phil Parkes, raced out of his area into the centre-circle and shouted to the Cosmos players: "Come on then, let's have you!" The crowd erupted and there were fans running onto the pitch, so the National Guard had to come out and surround us. It was very frightening. I was there with Parkes in the centre-circle with the National Guard all around us and it was 15-20 minutes before the game was re-started. We were too afraid to go back to the hotel at night in case there were fans waiting for us, so we collected our things early in the morning and flew out as soon as we could.

AFTER RETURNING FROM Vancouver, I signed for Burton Albion and then had a short spell at Belper Town before finishing with football completely. Football didn't thrill me enough to make me want to stay in the game. I didn't watch any games, even on TV, for about four years after retiring. I got a job as a newsagent and I was up early in the morning, so football took a back seat for a while.

After running the newsagents for about ten years, I then decided to look for something which wouldn't mean me having to get up early in the mornings because it took its toll after a while. We saw an advert for the Post Office at Hill Top in Eastwood, applied for it and got it. We've been here for about 16 years now, but the future of the Post Office is uncertain at the moment because it's scheduled for closure. There's a groundswell of people who want it to remain open and we're just getting carried along with it. It really is incredible how many people want to save it. There's going to be a public consultation and they'll see what objections they receive. If enough people object to the plans, they'll look at it again. There will be some compensation if it does shut, but it won't be as much as the business is worth.

I've been to games in the past when ex-players have been invited but it's not always possible because of problems associated with staff cover.

Derby's result is the first one I look for on a Saturday and the second one is Forest's. It makes my day if Derby have won and Forest have lost! We're right on the border of Derbyshire and Nottinghamshire and for the first few years we were in the Post Office, Forest were doing well in the old First Division while Derby were struggling, so I had it rubbed in my face. Things have changed a bit now, which is nice.

KEVIN WILSON
STRIKER 1979–1985

BORN 18 April 1961, Banbury
SIGNED December 1979 from Banbury United; £25,000
RAMS CAREER 141 games, 41 goals
HONOURS 42 Northern Ireland caps, 6 goals
LEFT Transferred to Ipswich Town, January 1985; £150,000

After making the switch from non-league football, Kevin found himself playing in the top-flight just a few months later. He initially struggled to adjust to the step-up before finding his feet. A prolific spell in front of goal led to his move to Ipswich and he later starred for Chelsea, establishing himself as a regular in the Northern Ireland team.

Derby County 5 v Hartlepool United 1

League Cup First Round, First Leg
Wednesday 29 August 1984

Baseball Ground
Attendance 9,281

Wilson fires four-goal salvo at the start of an impressive scoring spree

Teams

	Managers	
Arthur Cox		Billy Horner
Eric Steele	1	Michael Finch
Charlie Palmer	2	David Robinson
Steve Buckley	3	John Brownlie
Steve Powell	4	Graeme Hedley
Rob Hindmarch	5	Anthony Smith
Kenny Burns	6	John Bird
Kevin Taylor	7	Phil Brown
Kevin Wilson	8	Roy Hogan
Bobby Davison	9	Les Mutrie
Paul Hooks	10	Kevin Dixon
(Sub. Paul Richardson)		
John Robertson	11	Paul Dobson

	Scorers	
Wilson 5, 9, 54, 58		Hedley 43
Powell 87		

Referee: A Robinson

I PLAYED THREE RESERVE games for Sheffield United after signing on a three-year deal from Banbury. At that time Sheffield United had a surgeon who worked for the national side and he said that I'd got a problem with my knee, so they cancelled my contract and I went back to Banbury. It was a big disappointment to be turned down by Sheffield United because I wanted to be a professional footballer. The Banbury manager took me to Nuffield Hospital in Oxford and asked a specialist for his opinion on my knee. I was relieved when he told me that he'd give me 20 years in professional football.

Fortunately I was then spotted by Tim Ward, who is of course a legendary figure in Derby's history. He was a gentleman and a genuine bloke and you don't get many of them. A couple of weeks later, Derby took me for a week's trial. I scored three goals in a first-team versus reserves practice match which featured senior players like Roy McFarland, Bruce Rioch and Steve Buckley. I did enough to impress manager Colin Addison because Derby signed me for £25,000. I was 18. Unfortunately, it was a club which was going the wrong way at that time.

I scored in my first reserve game at Blackburn Rovers and four months later, I made my first-team debut as a substitute against Liverpool. You couldn't ask for a better debut really, coming on at Anfield, even though we were 3-0 down at the time. We were virtually certain of going down to the Second Division as well, but from a personal point of view it was a great start to my career.

I found my second season to be difficult because I'd spent the summer back home and I was a little bit home-sick. I was fortunate enough to go into digs in Ashbourne with a couple who knew my mum and dad, so I adjusted quite quickly after that. I found the full-time training hard initially and I remember Alan Ashman, who was the chief scout, saying that it might take me two years to settle down. Fortunately, I did settle down and did okay.

I was lucky enough to play and train with Kevin Hector. I was a similar player to him and I learned a lot from working with him, as I did with Alan Biley and Dave Swindlehurst, because you learn a bit from each player.

I didn't have the best of goalscoring records for the first few years at the club, but I hung in there and scored nine goals in 20 games in my third season. The fact that I was leading scorer that season showed that it was a club in turmoil, with all sorts of off-the-field issues. Charlie George returned to the club towards the end of that season and he was a larger than life character. He still had great ability and was someone you looked up to.

When John Newman replaced Addison as manager, nothing really changed because he didn't really bring anything different to the table. But when Peter Taylor came in there was a vast improvement in my game because he was very direct and very straight. However, apart from enjoying a good run in the FA Cup – when we knocked-out Forest 2-0 in the third round before I scored both goals in a 2-1 win over Chelsea – it was a bit of a downward spiral for the club.

WHEN ARTHUR COX TOOK over as manager, he gave me a direction because his man-management was excellent. He showed me the right direction, helping me improve mentally and physically, so I had a lot of time for him. Arthur drilled it into me that, as a striker, I had to be single-minded in order to score goals. When I came into the dressing room after scoring, he'd say, "Well, that's what you're paid to do." That's how he was.

I made a great start to the 1984/85 season, finding a rich vein of form in front of goal. And the game that really stands out was the League Cup first round, first leg, against Hartlepool, when I scored four goals in a 5-1 win. It was only the second game of the season, coming just four days after an opening day defeat at Bournemouth. But we were soon into our stride against Hartlepool, taking the lead in the fifth minute. Kenny Burns played a long pass to Bobby Davison who sent over a low cross and I nipped in ahead of a defender to turn the ball home at the near post. I was on target again four minutes later, taking advantage of an error from the goalkeeper who fluffed a goal-kick. The ball went straight to me and I just slid it past the keeper as he rushed out to try and rectify his mistake. Davison and Steve Buckley both fired in shots before we took our foot off the pedal towards the end of the half, letting Hartlepool pull a goal back just before the break. Buckley challenged Kevin Dixon for a cross and the ball fell to Graeme Hedley who had time and space to pick his spot.

Lifted by the goal, Hartlepool then had a couple of good chances to equalise. Paul Dobson chipped Eric Steele, only to see the ball go beyond the far post, while Les Mutrie fired over from a good position after getting the better of Kenny Burns. There weren't many who could say that because

Kenny was a whole-hearted player with a lot of ability and an incredible heart. You wouldn't want to meet him on a Saturday night! I was his chauffeur because he'd just got banned from driving. He had won the European Cup with Forest before following Peter Taylor down the A52 when he had walked out on Cloughie and taken over as Derby manager.

Any thoughts of Hartlepool staging a revival were effectively ended, however, when I completed my hat-trick to make it 3-1. John Robertson delivered an excellent cross after receiving a short free-kick from Buckley and I found the net with a header. 'Robbo' was absolute quality and he set up a lot of goals for me. I grabbed my fourth goal soon afterwards, beating John Brownlie to a ball from Davison before finishing with a chip from the edge of the box. Derby legend Steve Powell completed the scoring after meeting a cross from Buckley, who had a lovely left foot, to give us a sizeable lead to take into the second leg.

Everything seemed to click that night and scoring the four goals probably gave me the inspiration I needed at that stage of my career. When you're in that sort of form, you never expect to miss and the goal seems a lot bigger. I've still got the autographed match ball from the match. I got six hat-tricks in my career, but that was the only time I scored four goals. I then scored a hat-trick against Bolton the following Saturday. Unfortunately, I didn't get the match ball from that game because it got booted out of the ground at the end by one of the Bolton players. I'm still looking for it, if anyone knows where it is!

MY SCORING FORM continued with 13 goals in as many games, before suffering a broken arm against Plymouth. I came in on the Monday with my arm in plaster and Arthur Cox told me that I had to get back as soon as I could because Ipswich were going to buy me. Arthur was a very straight and honest man and I appreciated that.

My first game back was at Gillingham on Boxing Day and it wasn't long before I did sign for Ipswich. It was a difficult decision to leave Derby, but it was one that I had to make because I wanted to play at a higher level. Arthur was just as chuffed as anybody because he wanted me to go and play in the top-flight and it was a feather in his cap as well. He later tried to buy me back when I went to Chelsea, but they wouldn't sell me.

I had two years at Ipswich and I had a real good time there, scoring 25 goals one season, including two at Sunderland on the last day of the season to keep us up. The manager, Bobby Ferguson, and coach, Charlie Woods, really worked hard on me to improve my game. A lot of my game when I was younger was based on going in behind and turning defenders, but they taught me how to hold the ball up and bring others into play.

I then joined Chelsea and suffered relegation there after we lost to Charlton in the Play-offs. We came back up the following year, 1988/89, after going on a 27-match unbeaten run. Chelsea was a big club and it was a way of life you had to adjust to. It was a different experience, being able to go and see shows at night and see concerts at places like Wembley and Earl's Court. It was good from that point of view and being there probably furthered my career because I was a Northern Ireland international at that time. I played with some big characters like Vinnie Jones and Dennis Wise during my time at Stamford Bridge.

After finding myself in and out of the side, I became unsettled. Our kids were young as well, so we decided to move back nearer home. On transfer deadline day, I was away in Yugoslavia with Northern Ireland and Blackburn Rovers made an offer of £450,000 for me. The plane was delayed on the way back and didn't land at Heathrow until about 1.30pm. The chief scout was waiting for me at the airport and he told me that a bid from Blackburn had been accepted. The deal had to be done by 5.00pm and they wanted me to take a flight to Manchester at 2.30pm. The Blackburn manager, Don MacKay, really wanted me, but they'd left it too late. Jack Walker had started pumping money into the club, so I received a very good offer, but it wasn't about the money; I was more concerned with making sure that my family was okay.

I went to report for training at Chelsea on the Monday morning and was told to train with the youth team. They seemed to be blaming me for the deal not going through. But then I got a phone call on the Saturday morning telling me to join the first-team because someone had been taken ill and I scored against Luton that day. I then had a spell at Notts County where I fell out with Neil Warnock. There again, I think he falls out with everybody! I respected him as a manager, however, because you only have to look at his record. Neil's done a great job wherever he's been. I think I was the first one to wish him all the best when he got the sack at County.

I became player/coach at Walsall and later became manager of Northampton. I'd been Ian Atkins' assistant, so it was quite easy making the step up because I knew the players inside out. We won promotion and when I look back, I think that things happened too quickly for me. I made a few mistakes and lost my job.

I've managed at non-league level since leaving Northampton and I'm now at Corby Town in the Southern Premier League, with my old Derby team-mate Alan Biley as my assistant. He worked with me previously at Kettering. Alan and I were in digs together when we were at Derby, living in a place in St Chad's Road. Alan sort of took me under his wing, making sure I was looked after. If I needed any help, he was always there. When I made my debut at Anfield, for example, he came over to me, shook my hand and wished me all the best. That meant a lot really because Alan was a senior pro and I had a lot respect for him. I think we work together really well.

I was previously in charge of Kettering and there was a bit of a crazy time there when Gazza came in as manager. We were fourth in the table and were unbeaten in seven games without conceding a goal. We also reached the first round of the FA Cup for the first time in the history of the club. Then Gazza was given an opportunity and they wanted me to become Director of Football. I was basically pushed into the background, more or less operating as a chief scout, going to watch games and players. I wasn't involved in the training, which was something I was used to doing, day in, day out. I was bitter because the opportunity was taken from me at a time when I felt we were moving in the right direction. That year we could have been there or thereabouts regarding getting into the Conference.

When Gazza left after a controversial short spell, I made the silly mistake of going back. People say 'never go back' and they're right because I shouldn't have done. I'd changed and the players had changed. The bitterness was still in my mind and I should have turned down the offer because I had an offer to go to Holland to do some coaching at that time. I turned it down to return to Kettering and a little bit down the line I'm back to where I was before.

In between the two spells at Kettering, I was at Hucknall. The chairman of Hucknall is Brian Holmes, who used to be a director at Derby. I think we were fifth in the table when I was sacked following a poor performance at home to Farsley Celtic. I still speak to Brian and I think he looks back and realises it was a mistake. I certainly think it was a mistake because Hucknall have probably gone backwards as a club since then. Expectations were high at that time after they'd reached the FA Trophy final, but I thought the expectations were unrealistic. The club needs a bit stability and time for it to develop.

Now I am at Corby Town and I'd like to take them on and be successful and I think we can do it because we've had a lot of help from the Council and the board has got a vision of moving everything forward. I still have ambitions to get back into full-time management and I am doing my

Pro-Licence which will hopefully further my career because it's the highest level you can reach in coaching. My chairman at Corby Town, Peter Mallender, is also the chairman of Footballcv.com, which is a database of available players. I'm also involved in the organisation and we hold trials at various grounds. We arrange for a panel of scouts to come and take a look and sometimes they see somebody who attracts their interest. We've had a few success stories. The people involved in the organisation looked at forming an academy to push it forward and that's what has happened. It is unique because it's the first private academy in the world. I'm the team manager of the Footballcv Academy, which is based at Rushden & Diamonds. It's a very good set-up. The lads go to school in the morning and train in the afternoon. We've got a lot of plans. Long-term, we hope to have our own facilities and hopefully we can have a few more academies.

A lot of the lads are doing NVQs in sport. Being a footballer is a great job and that's what I keep telling the lads in the academy. You can't beat doing something you enjoy, day in, day out.

I'll always be thankful to Derby for giving me the opportunity to play football professionally. Derby was my first club and I have a fond affection for them. I married a Derby girl and it's a place where people are knowledgeable about football. When I look back on my time at the club, the only downside was that we weren't successful. From a professional point of view, it was a great place to start and when I left, I missed it. I made some good friends there and it was a really nice, friendly club.

PHIL GEE
STRIKER 1985–1992

BORN 19 December 1964, Pelsall
SIGNED September 1985 from Gresley Rovers; £5,000
RAMS CAREER 144 games, 31 goals
HONOURS Second Division Championship 1986/87
LEFT Transferred to Leicester City, March 1992 (exchange deal involving Ian Ormondroyd & Paul Kitson)

Phil was a pacy striker who forged an effective partnership with Bobby Davison after being plucked from non-league football. He scored 15 League goals in the 1986/87 season to help Derby win promotion to Division One as they enjoyed a revival under Arthur Cox, who christened him 'the next Ian Rush'. Following the arrival of big-money signings like Dean Saunders and Paul Goddard, Phil later found his first-team chances limited.

Sheffield United 0 v Derby County 1

League Division Two
Saturday 25 April 1987

Bramall Lane
Attendance 19,166

Gee goal sets new club-record and puts Rams
on the brink of a top-flight return

Teams

Billy McEwan	**Managers**	Arthur Cox
John Burridge	1	Eric Steele
Andy Barnsley	2	Paul Blades
Martin Pike	3	Mickey Forsyth
Martin Kuhl	4	Geraint Williams
(Sub. David Frain)		
Paul Stancliffe	5	Rob Hindmarch
Jeff Eckhardt	6	Ross MacLaren
Colin Morris	7	Gary Micklewhite
Steve Foley	8	Phil Gee
Peter Withe	9	Mark Lillis
Andy Kennedy	10	John Gregory
Peter Beagrie	11	Nigel Callaghan
	Scorer	Gee 69

Referee: M Reed

I PLAYED FOR THE local district side in Walsall when I was a kid and dreamed of becoming a professional footballer. I wrote to a few League clubs and a Plymouth scout replied, saying that he'd come and watch me play, but then I broke my toe and couldn't play for a few weeks. When I got to 17 and left school, I went on a YTS programme as a painter and decorator and thought my chance of becoming a professional footballer had gone.

After playing Sunday League football for a team called Riley Sports, I signed for Gresley Rovers in the summer of 1985 and scored six goals in five games at the start of the season. After my fifth appearance, which was on the August Bank Holiday Monday, I received a call from the manager the following night, informing me that Derby wanted to sign me. I didn't believe him, so I won't repeat what I said to him! I travelled to Derby on the Wednesday, had a medical the following day and signed on 2 September. It was just a whirlwind time for me because I'd gone from watching these players to training with them, all in a short space of time. I was a quiet lad and I was in awe of everybody.

When we played a game in my first training session, I tried chipping Mark Wallington, who was in the opposition goal. The ball hit the bar and I thought nothing of it until Mark came charging over to me when we were in the changing room afterwards. "Who do you think you are, trying to chip me?" he shouted. Facing such an experienced player who was apparently so irate, I shat myself and tried to push myself into the wall because I didn't know what I'd done. But Mark then started smiling and I realised he was having a bit of a laugh.

When I first came to the club, I was in digs with a fella called Steve McClaren. He was a good bloke and a decent, intelligent player whose range of passing was very good. I was involved in a couple of training sessions before playing for the reserves, away at Barnsley. I don't mind admitting that I was bricking it! But I managed to score a goal and we won 2-1. I made my first-team debut in the Freight-Rover Trophy, away at Brentford. Our reserve side played and we got a creditable 0-0 draw against their first-team.

My League debut was against my home-town club, Walsall, at the Baseball Ground in March 1986. I scored my first League goal in the penultimate game of the season against Rotherham after coming on as a sub in place of Geraint Williams, who we called 'George'. The 2-1 victory saw us clinch promotion to Division Two. We didn't have the best players, but we had a great team-spirit and that carried us through.

ARTHUR COX WAS A tough man who made us do a lot of running in training. He made it enjoyable though with five-a-side matches on Friday mornings. In the 1986/87 season, I struck up a good understanding with Bobby Davison who was the same type of player as me. When we started off playing together, we were going after the same balls, so it took a few games for us to get used to playing alongside each other. Mark Lillis, who had been bought from Manchester City, was in the side at the start of the season until he got injured in the game at home to Crystal Palace in early September. I came on in the League Cup against Chester and managed to get a goal with my first touch. Ross McLaren took a free-kick which bounced off someone and I smashed the ball home. But I didn't score for a while in the League and Lillis was well on the road to recovery when I finally found my touch, scoring six goals in seven games. Even when Mark was fit, the gaffer wouldn't drop me because he wasn't the type to change a winning team.

John Gregory was probably the star player at the time because he'd played for England and had made a lot of appearances in the First Division. Winger Nigel Callaghan had also dropped down a division to play for us. After losing the opening game of the 1986/87 season at home to Oldham, we started to do well, picking up some good results. We enjoyed a 13-match unbeaten run between January and April and went to Sheffield United at the end of that month knowing that victory would put us on the brink of promotion. John Burridge and Peter Withe, who I'd watched when I supported Aston Villa as a kid, were both in the Sheffield United side and to play against them so early in my career made it all the more memorable for me.

Bobby Davison was injured, so Mark Lillis was in the side alongside me. Mark was a different type of player who held the ball up rather than looked for balls played in the channel, like Bobby and myself did. Eric Steele had taken over in goal a few weeks earlier from Mark Wallington who'd dislocated a finger in the game at Ipswich. 'Steeley' was a good keeper who never let us down.

It was a stop-start game because referee Mike Reed kept blowing for everything. He gave a lot of free-kicks and wouldn't play the advantage,

which spoilt the flow of the game. If you looked at the statistics, we prob-
ably only actually played for about 50 minutes because Reed was blowing
his whistle all the time. As a result, there were few scoring chances. Eric
Steele made a couple of saves from Peter Withe. At the other end, Nigel
Callaghan tested John Burridge in the home goal. Burridge also kept out a
Mark Lillis effort with his legs after I'd headed down a free kick from Ross
MacLaren.

The all-important goal came midway through the second-half. We were
defending at the time, but I never used to go far back to defend because I
was a liability, so I was usually the player left upfield at corners. The ball
was played to Nigel Callaghan just outside the 'D' and he just cleared it. I
might be wrong, but I don't think he was looking for me. The ball went past
me, so I started running after it. United's Paul Stancliffe misjudged the
bounce of the ball, so I latched onto it, pushed it past him and ran onto it.
Burridge came off his line to around the penalty spot, but I didn't really
look at him because I just hit the ball and it went through his legs, which I
don't think he was happy about! I wasn't sure what to do after scoring
because I didn't have one of those rehearsed routines that you see sometimes; it was just a case of having my arms up in the air, jumping up and
down. The attendance was over 19,000 and I think about ten thousand were
our fans who filled the end behind that goal.

Incidentally, it was clear when we played Burridge's new club
Southampton the following season that he hadn't forgotten about the fact
that I'd scored against him at Bramall Lane. During the game at The Dell, I
pushed the ball past Burridge after he'd raced out of his area and he
chopped me down. After getting booked, he walked towards me as I
received treatment, bent down and said: "You won't do it again, you little
bastard."

The Blades tried desperately to force an equaliser, but without success.
Withe had an appeal for a penalty turned down, Colin Morris put two
efforts over the bar and Andy Kennedy struck the foot of a post, which
was the closest they came. We defended well though with Rob
Hindmarch and Ross MacLaren putting in strong performances in central
defence. We also competed well in midfield and in Gary Micklewhite we
had a winger who was a very good crosser of the ball. He wasn't someone
who'd try and show off on the wing with fancy tricks. If he could send
the ball over first time, that's what he'd do. That's great for a striker
because it's frustrating when you get a winger who keeps checking back
when you've made your run.

Sheffield United had Steve Foley sent-off eight minutes from time following a terrible challenge on George Williams. It was an assault, to be honest. That helped us as they couldn't make any headway with ten men and we held on for a famous victory. The result saw us set a new club record of 11 away wins after equalling the record the season before. The margin of victory was typical of how we performed that season because we managed to grind out results. There were four away matches where we won 1-0 and I scored the goal.

We only needed one point from the last three games to be absolutely certain of promotion.

As it was, we sealed it in the following game with a 2-1 win at home to Leeds. It was Bobby Davison's first game back after injury and we both scored.

We had a game away at Reading on the Monday to prepare for, so we were told to not go out drinking late on the Saturday night. Was that instruction followed? No, don't be daft! I went out with my landlord and his wife, visiting a few pubs on the outskirts of Derby. Then I got talked into going to a nightclub. I thought that I'd be safe if I went for about an hour, early on, so I could return to my digs for about 11.30pm. Nigel Callaghan, who was DJing in the club that night, got me to present some flowers to a girl who was celebrating her 21st birthday. Unfortunately, she later made a phone call to the club, as she wanted to place on record her thanks to me for the presentation, dropping me right in it! So after we lost 3-0 at Reading, I was called in to see Arthur Cox the following day and fined. To be fair, I shouldn't have gone to the nightclub, but I got carried away with the excitement of winning promotion to the First Division. After all, it doesn't happen every day!

WE WERE BROUGHT BACK down to earth with a bump the following season because it was very hard. I was in and out of the side at the start of the season. When we sold Bobby Davison to Leeds in November, I was pretty much playing up front on my own because we didn't really have another centre-forward. There was Andy Garner, but we only probably played together a couple of times. It would have been hard enough if I'd had a partner up there because the defenders were a lot quicker and they read the game a lot better.

We started to get some big-name players in with the likes of Peter Shilton and Mark Wright signing for the club. More money was spent the following season with Dean Saunders, Paul Goddard and Trevor Hebberd coming in and we managed to finish in fifth place. I was only playing infrequently by this stage and I was very frustrated. Quite often, I wasn't even on the bench, so it was a very frustrating time. I desperately wanted to play, but I don't think the gaffer would have picked me, however well I was playing in the reserves or however badly Saunders or Goddard were playing. He'd paid big money for them and had to justify it whereas I'd only cost about £5,000 and a box of Kit-Kats or something! Equally I couldn't understand why he wouldn't let me go out on loan. I used to let him know that I wasn't happy playing in the reserves and he'd tell me that no clubs had been in for me. I'd then trudge off, feeling even worse than when I went in.

Mick Harford came in during the 1989/90 season and I found him to be a very nice bloke. He was an honest player and I've got a lot of respect for him. We narrowly avoided relegation that season, finishing just a couple of places above the bottom three. I remained a bit-part player when we went down the following season. I probably wasn't training as hard because I knew I wasn't going to be involved. Things got so bad that I contemplated just packing in playing, but I managed to get my head together in pre-season and decided to give it another go. I thought that my chances of playing had improved following the transfer of Dean Saunders and I was ready to give it my all. I was out of contract that summer and I received calls from various managers who expressed interest in signing me, but I didn't want to leave Derby. I did well in pre-season and started the season in the team.

It was the start of a new era for the club because Lionel Pickering had bought the majority shareholding from Robert Maxwell. I played in the first eight games of the season before losing my place and it turned out to be a stop-start time for me again. I scored twice against Aston Villa in the Cup and that turned out to be my last appearance for the Rams. Arthur Cox was looking to build a team with Lionel Pickering's money and he brought in Marco Gabbiadini to play up front. I was surplus to requirements so I was allowed to go to Leicester with Ian Ormondroyd in a deal which took Paul Kitson to Derby.

I was sad to go but I had to leave because it was obvious I wasn't part of the gaffer's plans. Some people have a go at me even now for going to Leicester, but I didn't go there to annoy Derby County fans. I went there purely and simply because they gave me an opportunity to go and play first-team football.

AT THE END OF THe 1991/92 season, Leicester lost to Blackburn in the Play-off final and we got to the Play-off final again the following year, losing to Swindon. The year after, we again reached the final where we faced, yes, Derby, although I didn't play that day. At the start of the 1992/93 season, I had scored six goals in eight games before getting injured. After missing four games, I got my fitness back and was raring to go, but I didn't get picked. That was really frustrating after the way I'd started the season, full of confidence and in good form. The manager, Brian Little, decided against recalling me and my confidence just dropped. At the end of that season, I had a dig at Little when we were on a pre-season trip. I told him that I'd got a new position for myself in the team. After a few drinks, I told him: "You've got a left-back and a left-winger. I'm the best left-out you've ever signed!" I apologised to him when we got back, but it didn't help me because I still didn't get picked much after that.

I got injured in the 1995/96 season during a reserve match at Port Vale. I damaged my cartilage, so I had an operation to try and cure it. But every time I tried to make a comeback, my knee blew up with all the fluid in it. Martin O'Neill had taken over from Mark McGhee as manager by then and he told me that he wanted me to join in with the training. I told him that my knee didn't feel right but I went out to train and when I turned, I ripped my cartilage again. I was told to rest and I could only watch as the lads finally won promotion via the Play-offs, with Steve Claridge shinning in the winning goal in the last minute of extra-time in the Wembley final against Crystal Palace. I spoke to the gaffer about my situation after the Play-off final because I was out of contract and feared that I was going to get released. He said: "Don't worry about that tonight, you'll be all right." I was quite happy because I thought he was going to give me another contract.

A couple of days later, O'Neill called me into his office and asked me how my knee was. "It's not the best," I replied. "Well, I've got to let you go," he said. I was very, very disappointed with that. Hereford manager Graham Turner wanted to sign me, so I went there, sorted out a contract and underwent a medical. The specialist said straight away that there was something wrong with my left knee. Graham told me to get it sorted out, so I came back to have surgery in Derby. It turned out that I'd torn my cartilage again and a few months later the surgeon came to the conclusion that I couldn't take full-time training. That's when I had to pack in playing professionally. I felt very bitter towards Leicester City because other players have been helped while they recover from injury. All I was told was that I could train at the training ground after all the other players had gone, which I wasn't very happy about.

I went to train at Hednesford, but I couldn't even carry on playing at non-league level because my knee just wouldn't take it.

I had to start working, so I went back to decorating. My first job was for the former Sheffield Wednesday goalkeeper Kevin Pressman, doing his hallway, landing and stairs. The physio at Leicester, Alan Smith, worked with Kevin at Wednesday and he put him onto me. I was self-employed, but I've recently gone on the books of a builder I do a lot of work for. I did plan to go on a course to learn to be a physio, but that plan was ruined when I had to quit at the age of 31 because I had to earn a living. With a family and a mortgage to pay for, I just couldn't afford to take the time off to do the course.

I've retained links with football by doing some scouting. I scouted for Wolves when I first packed in, working for my old Leicester manager, Mark McGhee. When he left Molineux, I continued scouting for his successor, Colin Lee, and spent four years doing that. George Foster was then made chief scout and because he lived in Derby, he said that they didn't need two scouts in the same area, so I had to go. I got in touch with Mark McGhee again at Millwall and I started doing a bit for him.

I then got a call from Northampton's chief executive who told me that their manager, former Rams striker Kevin Wilson, needed a kit manager. He asked me if I'd like to do it and I took the job on for a season. It was a part-time role which involved organising the collection of the kit for washing, putting it away and making sure it was ready for matches. I quite enjoyed doing it, to be honest. I'm now doing some scouting for Blackpool who are managed by my old Leicester team-mate, Simon Grayson. I only do games for him when a team they're due to face are playing in my neck of the woods because they can't afford to send me all over the place.

I live in the Oakwood area of Derby and I sometimes play for the ex-Rams side. It's great to meet up with some of the old players. We also get together every Christmas for an ex-Rams do. It's great to be involved still.

MARCO GABBIADINI
STRIKER 1992–1997

BORN   20 January 1968, Nottingham
SIGNED   January 1992 from Crystal Palace; £1 million
RAMS CAREER   210 games, 60 goals
HONOURS   1 England 'B' cap, 2 England Under-21 caps
LEFT   Released, June 1997

After making his name at Sunderland as a prolific goalscorer, Marco endured a brief, unhappy spell at Crystal Palace before Arthur Cox shelled out £1 million to bring him to the Baseball Ground. He played a key role in Jim Smith's promotion-winning side, forging a successful strike-partnership with Dean Sturridge. After leaving Derby, Marco went on to play for a number of clubs, taking his tally of League goals past the 200 mark.

Derby County 3 v Sunderland 1

League Division One
Saturday 23 December 1995

Baseball Ground
Attendance 16,882

*Gabbiadini skippers Rams to victory over former club
in promotion battle*

Teams

Jim Smith	**Managers**	Peter Reid
Russell Hoult	1	Alec Chamberlain
Chris Powell	2	Dariusz Kubicki
Shane Nicholson	3	Martin Scott
Darryl Powell	4	Steve Agnew
		(sub. Gareth Hall)
Dean Yates	5	Martin Gray
		(sub. David Kelly)
Igor Stimac	6	Andy Melville
Sean Flynn	7	Michael Gray
Dean Sturridge	8	Richard Ord
Ron Willems	9	Craig Russell
(sub. Paul Simpson)		
Marco Gabbiadini	10	Phil Gray
Lee Carsley	11	Martin Smith
		(sub. Sam Aiston)

Gabbiadini 35, Willems (pen) 64 **Scorers**   M. Gray 34
Sturridge 84

Referee: P Richards

I STARTED OUT AT York under manager Denis Smith and then followed him to Sunderland when I was 19. I went from playing regularly playing in front of crowds of 3,000 to 20,000, so it was a good place for me to learn as a young player. Sunderland were at their lowest ebb after dropping down to the Third Division. I had a dream start, scoring six goals in my first four games. We won promotion straight away and managed to get back into the top-flight a couple of years later.

I'd been linked with Manchester United and a host of other top clubs before making a £1.8 million move to Crystal Palace, which turned out to be a very short and sweet affair. It was a strange carry on. When I look back, I think I should probably have gone to a bigger club than Palace. They'd got to the top-flight and reached the Cup final, with players like Eric Young, Andy Gray, Eddie McGoldrick and Geoff Thomas, who'd not done so well elsewhere and then flourished together. I went to Palace at the wrong time really because when I went into the dressing room, they all wanted to be away. At that time, the only way you made money was to get transferred because if you came through the ranks at a club, you had to keep adding years onto your contract to get a pay-rise. I was brought in to replace Ian Wright, who'd just moved to Arsenal, but I was a totally different player to him because I wanted the ball deeper at feet and to run at people and they played very much route one. My first impression was that others were desperate to get away. I was a big signing and my wages reflected that. I wouldn't say there was any bad feeling from the other players but they all wanted to improve the wages they were on. Steve Coppell's parting message to me was that he was very sorry it hadn't worked out, adding that he hadn't actually seen me play before signing me, which was a bit bizarre!

I ended up at Derby quite quickly. Lionel Pickering had come in and I was the first million pound signing. I took a bit of a gamble, dropping down a division, but I think the Derby fans took to me pretty quickly. I thought it had paid off just a few months later when we had a great win towards the end of the season, only just missing out on promotion. At 4.40pm on the last Saturday of the season, we were in a promotion spot because Middlesbrough were 1-0 down at Wolves before winning 2-1 with a goal in the last minute to go up instead of us.

We played Blackburn in the Play-offs and we were 2-0 up at their place in the first leg before losing 4-2. We were winning 2-0 again in the return leg before they came back to level and then Kevin Moran scored the winner with a header which just bobbled in. It was a shocking goal and it really gutted us.

We then had a couple of seasons where we couldn't get it together at all. We had a really good side, but we lacked a bit of experience. The lads who came in – such as Tommy Johnson, Paul Kitson and Mark Pembridge – were all young. Most of the lads went on to great things, but it was maybe a case of having too many young players in the side at that time.

We got to the final of the Anglo-Italian Cup at Wembley in the 1992/93 season and I scored, which was my only goal at the stadium. Wembley was the unluckiest place in the world for me because I was on the losing side six times there, I think.

THE FOLLOWING SEASON, we got to the Play-off final against Leicester, which was a memorable game for the wrong reasons after losing 2-1. We should have beaten them, to be honest. Arthur Cox packed in during the early part of that season because he was having trouble with his back. Roy McFarland is a smashing guy and one of the most genuine blokes you could meet, but he didn't really stamp his authority on the team because things carried on like they had done under Arthur. We had a £30million squad, so to not even make the Play-offs in the 1994/95 season was poor. We should have achieved more than we did.

Jim Smith, who took over in the summer of 1995, was very old school, but he did bring in the new techniques. He also made a few signings and all the old ways were forgotten, so it was nice for someone new to come in and clear the decks. Saying that, I was out of contract that summer, so I was a little nervous at one point when he started letting a few players go.

Jim was clever in the transfer market, bringing in the likes of Robbie van der Laan, Gary Rowett and Ronnie Willems. We didn't have a massive change around in squad, but with a new coach in Steve McClaren, things were different. Jim gave Steve licence to try out new techniques and training was enjoyable. There was more work on technical matters and more fitness work. There were times when Jim wouldn't be at training for a couple of days. He'd fly off to Milan to visit training grounds and check on other methods. He takes a lot of credit for embracing new ideas and letting Steve, who was unproven, have his head. It was an interesting time.

We had a ropey start, failing to win in the first four games. We were in the bottom three in October, so we were really struggling and Jim could have easily been sacked. We got stuffed 5-1 at Tranmere in Igor Stimac's first game after signing, but then we had a really good run after that, winning ten out of 11 games to climb the table.

I'VE CHOSEN THE home game against Sunderland as my Match of My Life because we began the day behind them in second place and replaced them at the top of the table after winning, so it was a huge game. Another reason why it was such a special game for me is because I was made captain for the day against my former club. I think Robbie van der Laan was suspended or injured, so I captained the side for a few games. I was one of the longest-serving players at the club and I'd captained other clubs, so I was more than happy to take on the role.

We went behind when Shane Nicholson only half-cleared Martin Smith's corner and Michael Gray fired past Russell Hoult from the edge of the area. We equalised straight from the kick-off. Dean Sturridge ran right through the middle and their players expected him to pass, but he just kept going. He got to the edge of the box, managed to slip me in and I fired in a shot which Alec Chamberlain got a hand to but couldn't keep out.

Sean Flynn smacked a shot against the post before we took the lead. Lee Carsley put Sturridge through and he was brought down in the area by Richard Ord. The referee had no hesitation in awarding a penalty which was put away by Ron Willems. Sunderland put us under pressure and they went desperately close to forcing an equaliser. Michael Gray's cross was met by Phil Gray and the ball was heading for the net until Russell Hoult pulled off a superb reaction save to keep it out. It was such a crucial save which must have really deflated the Sunderland players.

The game wasn't over, though, because Sunderland continued to put us under pressure as they tried to force an equaliser. But their hopes of taking at least a point were dashed when Sturridge made it 3-1 late on after I set him up. It was a massive win for us and kept our run going.

Dean, who scored some good goals that year, was a funny player. We all knew he had potential, but he was always injured when he was young because he was sort of too strong for his own body. He used to pull his hamstrings constantly and they eventually worked out that it was all to do with him building up his thighs. He used to build his thighs up and when he then went out to sprint, his thighs were pulling his hamstrings off. They stopped him doing that and made him work generally on his fitness. Once he stopped getting injured, he began to realise his potential. Dean was very confident and quite an arrogant lad, which I don't think he'll mind me saying.

Dean Yates, who had an excellent game that day, was a good defender who was very unlucky with injuries in his career. Darryl Powell and Lee Carsley had good games in midfield. Lee had just made the breakthrough that season. He was a good young player and he's gone on to have a great career.

In Russell Hoult, we had a good keeper. Before substitute goalkeepers were allowed, he was at Leicester when the first-choice keeper got injured in the warm-up and they had to put out a Tannoy announcement, asking for Russell to report to the dressing room. He was just tucking into a massive hot dog at the time, so 'Hot Dog' was his nick-name from then on. Everyone played a part that season. Ron Willems was a good footballer and a lovely guy. Sadly, I understand he's now in an asylum back in his native Holland. Igor Stimac, who was a really nice guy, came in and had that arrogance. Gary Rowett was a revelation and Robbie van der Laan was a character. You always knew he was a good player when you played against Robbie at Port Vale, but I was a little surprised when he was made captain as soon as he came into the dressing room. But to be honest, it was a masterstroke really. We had a good dressing room and a good social thing going on, so it was a good club to come to. The wives and girlfriends also used to mix together as well.

I scored in the last minute against Norwich at the Baseball Ground on New Year's Day and the atmosphere that day was awesome. It was an exciting year for us because we knew we had to go up as the Premiership was beginning to become more important. We had a stutter just before spring, drawing a lot of games, while Crystal Palace put together a late run, so they were in good form when we faced them at the Baseball Ground in the penultimate game of the season. It was a really huge game because we knew that we'd miss out if they beat us. We sealed promotion, however, with a 2-1 win.

Ashley Ward came in for the last game of the campaign against West Brom and you could see that Jim Smith was planning for the following season. We had a bit of a fall out over that because it was the last hurrah at the end of a long, hard season and I wanted to play. As it turned out, I was in and out of the team in the 1996/97 season and it turned out to be a bad year. I went on loan to Birmingham after initially saying that I didn't want to go. Birmingham manager Trevor Francis refused to take no for an answer. He kept ringing me and telling me that he wanted to take me on loan. "If you want me, I'd love to sign for you, but I don't want to go out on loan," I told him. "You know what I can do." I eventually did agree to go there on loan and I did my cartilage in my second week at the club. Then, of course, they're not interested in you as soon as you're injured.

I struggled to get fit towards the end of the season before going on loan to Oxford. That was also an unhappy time out on loan because in the month I was there, I think we lost five games. I was out of contract at the end of the season and it wasn't renewed so it was a bit of a sad end to my time at Derby.

I WENT TO GREECE to play for Panionios in Athens and the football was okay there. I scored about half a dozen goals in around 20 games, but unfortunately they weren't very good at paying your wages over there. I got a chance to play for Stoke, so I came back to England. The problem was that I was in dispute with Panionios, through FIFA, over unpaid wages, so I signed a loan agreement because I couldn't sign a full-time contract. Stoke had made a good start to the season and were in the top six, but they were on a losing run when I joined in December and in the first month I was there, they sacked manager Chic Bates and brought in Chris Kamara as his replacement. Kamara didn't fancy me and he tried to get rid of me. I'd negotiated a contract with Stoke and signed a pre-agreement while the wrangling with Panionios was going on. Then their club secretary was diagnosed with cancer and dropped dead in my first fortnight there, so I didn't receive a copy of the letter. It really was a terrible time for all concerned.

While Stoke were still managerless I remember our game against Bradford City was shown live on Sky Sports and Kamara, who was co-commentating on the game, absolutely slaughtered the team. Then he came in as manager the next day, which was quite surreal! Kamara told us that we all started on an equalling footing and then he asked to speak to me after the meeting. "I'm sorry, when your contract's up, you can go," he said. I'd got really fit and my knee was good so it was really frustrating because I knew I could have done a good job for him. I sort of knew Kamara after having dinner with him and a mutual friends a few years before, but he didn't say anything like "nice to see you again" or anything. He just told me straight away that he'd be letting me go.

We agreed a settlement and I went back to York who were doing quite well in the third tier. I got injured in my first game, doing my ankle really badly, and I think the chairman thought I'd pulled a fast one, joining the club with an injury, so I wasn't offered anything at the end of the season.

That left me without a club a year after leaving Derby. I ended up at Darlington and scored 56 goals in two seasons there. It was frustrating because I was in the bottom league and I knew that I could have been playing much higher. I managed to get a three-year contract at Northampton a division higher. The club was experiencing financial problems at the time, so we went a few months without getting paid.

I FINISHED OFF PLAYING for Hartlepool, which I really enjoyed. My wife and I had bought a hotel in York by then, so it worked out well because Hartlepool was within easy travelling distance. When the kids were all in school, my wife Debbie wanted to do something, so we decided to run our own business. Both our parents ran hotels and York is of course a big tourist area, so we decided to buy Bishop's Hotel. It's been a challenge because there are days when it can be quite intense. We bought a place that was bigger than we originally planned. We've renovated the place and we've enjoyed the project management side of the business. It's an all-year-round business because there are only really a couple of weeks when we're quiet. It's a good business but I'm ready for another challenge now.

After retiring from playing, I needed a break from football, to be honest. I was lucky that we had a business which was up and running because I think some people stay in the game out of necessity. That shows sometimes in the way that they manage and the way they react to certain situations. It's been nice to step away from the game and have a break after playing nearly 800 games, playing week in, week out for 20 years. I think the longest I was ever out injured was about five weeks because I never had a serious injury.

When I first stopped playing, to have a Saturday afternoon off was a funny feeling, but quite enjoyable. We've got an apartment in Spain and we enjoy a nice lifestyle, so for the first couple of years, it wasn't such a big thing. But I've started to miss football now and it's possible that I could get involved in the game again. Every time a new season kicks off, I'll be sat there on a beach somewhere, reading a paper, thinking to myself that I'd have been preparing for the big kick-off for the last six weeks.

I think I'd be good at coaching or management because I can get my opinions across whereas a lot of managers can't string a sentence together. Some of them in the game aren't particularly good at the job but chairmen keep employing them just because of the fact that they've done it for so long.

We've taken on some new staff at the hotel who've taken a lot of the responsibility away from us. We've got four young kids, so I was happy to pick them up from school and be involved in everything they were doing. It was nice to be around them at that time. Now, as the kids are getting older, we're considering other avenues.

I could get involved in media work. You hear some of the lads on the radio who aren't very good. They just want to be nice to everyone, but you can't be nice to everyone. You've got to have an opinion, one way or the other. It's a lot to do with being in the right place at the right time with those sort of jobs. I'm out on a bit of limb at York as far as football is concerned and I don't live near either of my two main former clubs, Derby or Sunderland.

I really enjoyed my time at Derby and I hope I'm fondly remembered by the supporters. I went to watch the Play-off final against West Brom and received a good reception from the fans.

I always compare Derby with Sunderland because they're one-club towns and you don't get a lot of supporters from other areas. Everyone in Derby supports the club. They might not come to all the matches, but if something good is happening, the whole town is affected by it and it was good to be part of that.

MICHAEL JOHNSON
DEFENDER 2003-PRESENT

BORN   4 July 1973, Nottingham
SIGNED August 2003 from Birmingham City; undisclosed fee
RAMS CAREER 146 games, 5 goals *as at start of 2007/08 season
HONOURS   14 Jamaica caps, Anglo-Italian Cup 1995

Johnno is an experienced defender whose whole-hearted approach to the game has made him a popular figure with the fans. He was club captain during the 2006/07 season, but injuries limited his appearances as Derby secured promotion via the Play-offs. Despite missing out on a place in the match-day 16 at Wembley, Michael lifted the Championship Play-off trophy aloft with team skipper Matt Oakley.

Derby County 4 v Nottingham Forest 2

The Championship
Saturday 20 March 2004

Pride Park
Attendance 32,390

Victory over arch-rivals boosts Rams' survival hopes

Teams

George Burley	**Managers**	Joe Kinnear
Lee Grant		Barry Roche
Jeff Kenna		Michael Dawson
Richard Jackson		Wes Morgan
(sub. Paul Boertien)		
Youl Mawene		Matthieu Louis-Jean
Michael Johnson		Danny Sonner
Tom Huddlestone		Gareth Williams
Ian Taylor		Eoin Jess
Leon Osman		Andy Reid
Candido Costa		Andy Impey
(sub. Lee Holmes)		
Paul Peschisolido		Gareth Taylor
Marcus Tudgay		Nick Barmby
		(sub. David Johnson)
Taylor 4, Tudgay 82	**Scorers**	Taylor 45, Williams 67
Peschisolido 28, 37		

Referee: D Pugh

WHEN I WAS ASKED TO pick out a memorable game I played in for Derby, I had no hesitation in going for the win over Nottingham Forest in 2004. Now it's a bit different because I'm actually a Forest fan and I watched them as a kid growing up in Nottingham, although I signed for their neighbours across the River Trent, Notts County. When I played for Nottingham City Boys, a coach from County called Mick Walker offered me a trial, so I went there and signed for them straight away.

I later moved to Birmingham, where I spent eight years, before joining Derby in the summer of 2003. The Forest match came towards the end of my first season at the club. The fact that I lived in Nottingham, supported Forest and played for Derby rubbed a quite a few people up the wrong way, so I got quite a bit of stick for months before the game. I couldn't get away from it because loads of my mates are Forest fans and I also heard Forest fans joking about Derby on my local radio station.

We were in the bottom three at the time and Forest weren't doing so well either, so there was a lot resting on the outcome of the match. Apart from that, there's also pride at stake when you face your local rivals. Even though we were both battling to stay up, a lot of fans were more concerned about beating the arch-enemy than avoiding relegation! If you can't get up for a local derby, there's something wrong because fans thrive on them and you've got to try a bit harder than usual.

I didn't really know what to expect because it was my first game against Forest for Derby, but I soon found out after running out onto the pitch. The atmosphere was electric and you struggled to hear a team-mate who was only standing about ten yards away. The rivalry has obviously been there for years, but even though I was born and brought up in Nottingham, I didn't realise how intense it was until I played in my first derby.

Ian Taylor scored early on when he ran on to a ball from Paul Peschisolido before firing low past Barry Roche in the Forest goal. 'Tayls' had a great engine and could get from box to box. When he was at Aston Villa, he'd make late, surging runs into the box and that's what he did for us. On so many occasions he popped up with a goal to get us going or keep us in a game.

We went further ahead following the most bizarre goal I've ever witnessed. It's fame still lives on today! Wes Morgan played a back-pass to Roche, the ball hit a Kenco Coffee cup which had somehow found its way onto the pitch and bobbled up and went over Roche's foot as he went to kick it, bouncing off his shin and allowing 'Pesch' to run past him and tap the ball into the empty net. Even though I was some way from the action, I saw the ball take what appeared to be a massive bobble off the turf. It was only later that we all realised it had hit a coffee cup which is now in the trophy room at Pride Park. I don't know who retrieved the cup, but it's in there, signed by Pesch.

Even though less than half-an-hour had gone, Forest boss Joe Kinnear felt that he had to make a change, which was flattering, sending on strker David Johnson in place of Nick Barmby. Pesch scored again to make it 3-0 after linking up well with Marcus Tudgay, so we were on our way to a good victory. Pesch had made a good start to his Derby career after signing from Sheffield United and it was his fourth goal in three games for us. He's always been one of those players who'll just keep going and he's scored goals everywhere he's been, like a little annoying rat and he annoyed Forest that day.

Forest pulled a goal back just before the break when Gareth Taylor scored with a far post header. Then Gareth Williams made it 3-2 midway through the second-half, finding the net at the second attempt after his initial header came back off the bar. The two goals we conceded over-shadowed what had been a great performance, but we still felt comfortable at that stage because we knew we had enough in our locker to go on and win the game.

Pesch missed a chance to complete his hat-trick before Tudgay scored our fourth with just eight minutes left. Pesch scampered down the left and found Tudgay whose shot took a deflection to deceive Roche. Tudgay is not the biggest of centre-forwards, but he's got a great attitude with a never-say-die spirit, so he's a handful for defenders.

IT WAS THE FIRST TIME Derby had scored four goals against Forest for over 24 years. We absolutely battered them. It was a victory which will live in my memory for years. That's the same for the Derby fans, I'm sure, because they'd waited so long for a result like that against Forest. It was not only the fact that we won but the manner in which we beat them. A lot of people went to work on the Monday morning with a great big grin on their face. The whole city was absolutely bouncing! My mates who support Forest were fine with me because they realised that their team didn't perform on the day and that the better team won.

Leon Osman, who was on loan from Everton, had a good game that day. 'Ossie' was quality and he was probably the main reason why we stayed up that season because he scored some important goals as well as contributing to others. It's no surprise to me that he's a regular in the Everton side because he's a very good player. He's the first to admit that the season he had at Derby kick-started his career.

Youl Mawéné was my central defensive partner and he won the Player of the Year award that season. We also had Jeff Kenna in defence. He's been there and done it, winning the Premiership with Blackburn and playing in the top-flight for most of his career, as well as winning many caps for the Republic of Ireland. He was an important cog in our team and played a key role for us.

In midfield there was Candido Costa and Tom Huddlestone. Candido was a bag of tricks who made a massive contribution, going past players at will. He was Portuguese and a real likeable lad. Tom's passing range is exemplary and some people were talking about him being the next big thing in English football at that time because he had got the lot. He's still young and still learning his trade at Tottenham, so I think he has a great chance of being an England regular in the future.

Paul Boertin, who came on as a substitute against Forest, is one of those players who'll run through a brick wall for you. He'd spill blood for Derby because he's black and white through and through and that's probably why he's had so many injuries.

We remained in the bottom three after the win over Forest, but the result gave us a massive psychological lift as we approached a crucial part of the season. We proved that we could score goals and everyone was buzzing on the back of that performance. As it turned out, we finished a solitary point above the relegation zone, so the victory over Forest proved to be vital. You could go as far as saying that if we'd been relegated that season, we wouldn't be where we are today.

GEORGE BURLEY WAS THE manager at that time, having been appointed at the end of March 2003 after John Gregory left the club, and he turned things round the following season, taking us to the Play-offs, which speaks volumes for him. George is a good manager who made one or two cute signings and nearly got us into the Premiership. We just fell at the final hurdle, losing to Preston in the semi-finals of the Play-offs. We lost 2-0 in the first leg at Preston, following a couple of unfortunate errors. We were caught out by a long-ball for the first goal and then Lee Camp let an effort slip through his hands for the second. We had an uphill battle at Pride Park and gave it our best shot, but it wasn't to be.

Grzegorz Rasiak and Inigo Idiakez were key players for us that season. Grzegorz was an unknown quantity when he signed and a lot of defenders struggled to contain him. Inigo scored so many goals and also created goals from dead-ball situations. If we had a free-kick about 30 yards out, everyone knew that he'd at least test the goalkeeper.

There was a change of management in the summer of 2005 when George parted company with the club. Things like that happen in football and it's the type of thing that we as footballers have no control over. We had to move on and do the best we could for Derby County.

Phil Brown was named as the new manager and it was a difficult time for everyone. It was Phil's first managerial job, having been a successful coach at Bolton under Sam Allardyce, and a lot had happened at the club over the previous 12 months. People at the club, including the players, were coming to terms with that. After Phil left, Terry Westley did a good job as caretaker-manager towards the end of the season, saving us from relegation. The impact he made was second to none. He wanted the job full-time, but it wasn't to be.

Darren Moore, who arrived from West Brom that season, was quality. He was a big vocal presence on and off the field, giving the team a lot of guidance. I've got all the time in the world for 'Mooro' because he's top-class and a good bloke to have around. I knew him for some years before he came to Derby because we played together for Jamaica.

Billy Davies came in during the summer of 2006. His record at Preston was impressive and the passion he shows was one of the qualities that prompted the Board to go after him. It was a big achievement for us when we went up via the Play-offs at the end of Billy's first season in charge. To even be in the Play-offs was fantastic given our position the previous season.

Derby County deserve Premiership football, although there's no getting away from the fact that it's difficult because if you've been out of the top-flight for a number of years, you find that the gulf is even wider than it was before.

It's been a great roller-coaster ride for the players, fans and everyone involved with the club.

I've always had a great relationship with the Derby fans because I think they appreciate that I've always given them 100 per cent honesty. It's a fantastic club with a great tradition and I'm just glad that I've been part of the history of the club.

DARREN MOORE
DEFENDER 2006–PRESENT

BORN 22 April 1974, Birmingham
SIGNED January 2006 from West Brom; £500,000
RAMS CAREER 56 games, 5 goals *as at start of 2007/08 season
HONOURS 3 Jamaica caps

Darren is a rugged centre-back, with a huge physical presence, who was signed by Phil Brown at the end of his ill-fated spell in charge to bolster a struggling Derby team. Under caretaker-manager Terry Westley, he helped the Rams avoid relegation in 2005/06 and then played a key role the following season as they won promotion to the Premiership via the Play-offs.

Derby County 1 v West Bromwich Albion 0

Championship Play-off Final
Monday 28 May 2007

Wembley Stadium
Attendance 74,993

Pearson's first goal for Rams clinches return to Premiership

Teams

Billy Davies	**Managers**	Tony Mowbray
Stephen Bywater		Dean Kiely
Tyrone Mears		Paul McShane
		(sub. Nathan Ellington)
Dean Leacock		Chris Perry
Darren Moore		Sam Sodje
		(sub. Neil Clement)
Jay McEveley		Paul Robinson
Craig Fagan		Jason Koumas
(sub. Marc Edworthy)		
Matt Oakley		Jonathan Greening
Seth Johnson		Zoltan Gera
(sub. David Jones)		(sub. Darren Carter)
Stephen Pearson		Robert Koren
Steve Howard		Diomansy Kamara
Paul Peschisolido		Kevin Phillips
(sub. Giles Barnes)		

Pearson 61	**Scorer**	

Referee: G Poll

I SAID FROM THE age of nine or ten growing up in Birmingham that I wanted to be a professional footballer and my family gave me great support, helping me pursue a career in the game. I'm also grateful to the managers and coaches who had belief in me and allowed me to express my talent, right from youth level to where I'm at now.

I had three years as a pro at Torquay and then spent a similar amount of time at Doncaster. It was quite a slog in the lower divisions, but I wouldn't change anything because it was a good grounding in football for me. It gave me a great appetite for the game, which I still have. I went to Bradford City and won promotion to the Premiership with them. It was great to be part of that team because we had a fantastic time. I then had 18 months at Portsmouth, which was a great club, before spending five years at West Brom, where I was part of two promotion-winning sides.

Phil Brown signed me for Derby, but he left just four days later. I signed on the Thursday, Derby lost in the FA Cup at Colchester on the Saturday and then he was sacked on the following Monday, so I didn't really get much chance to know him. It was quite a difficult time for me, seeing the manager who signed me sacked within days, but I had to get on with the job in hand.

When I arrived at Derby, they were down at the foot of the table and we only had seven or eight weeks left to try and keep the club in the Championship. Terry Westley, who stood in as caretaker-manager, did a magnificent job under very difficult circumstances. He did really well to step up from his post in the Academy and work wonders as a manager. He managed to keep the club in the Championship and laid the foundations for Billy Davies. The gaffer brought in the likes of Stevie Howard, Gary Teale, Stephen Bywater, Matt Oakley, Jay McEveley and Stephen Pearson, who all proved to be astute signings. They all added to the team as well as being great characters in the dressing room.

AT THE START OF THE 2006/2007 season, the thought was that we'd try and get off to a good start and then see how far we could go. It was around Christmas time when we started thinking that we had just as good a chance as anybody of going up. We were on course to win automatic promotion before experiencing a bit of a wobble towards the end of the season, losing against Ipswich and drawing against Leicester and Coventry. They were tough games because Leicester and Coventry were fighting to avoid relegation and teams like that don't just hand it to you on a plate.

We obviously wanted to go up automatically, but that wasn't to be so we had a second bite of the cake in the Play-offs. A lot of people were writing us off, saying that we had no chance after blowing automatic promotion when we'd been in such a good position. But we won 2-1 in a great match at Southampton and then came through a tremendous game in the return leg to reach the final on penalties after Saints had won the game 3-2 on the night. That just goes to show the character of the team.

It was just a shame for me personally that I was playing against my old club in the final. It was hard because I was playing West Brom in a Play-off final a year after leaving the club; all my old team-mates and the staff I knew so well were there. West Brom is a fantastic club and I had five really great years there. I could imagine what was going through the minds of players like Paul Robinson, Zoltan Gera, Jason Koumas, Neil Clement and Jonathan Greening. But I had to give Derby my full commitment, of course, because, as a professional, you just have to get on with it.

It was a tremendous atmosphere at the new Wembley stadium and it turned out to be a very tight game in which there wasn't much time and space for either team. As early as the first minute, Stephen Bywater was forced to make a good save to keep out an effort from Diomansy Kamara. 'Bys' had a great season after signing from West Ham. He deserves a lot of credit because he was out of shape when he arrived at the club but he was focused and got himself into shape. He actually told me in his first week or two at the club that he was going to play in the Premiership with the team.

Albion appealed for a penalty in the tenth minute when Tyrone Mears nicked the ball off Koumas. At the time, I thought to myself: "I've seen them given", but I have to take my hat off to Graham Poll, who was taking charge of his last ever game as a referee, because replays of the incident showed that he was right on the spot to make the correct decision. It was a great tackle by Tyrone, who was magnificent on the day. They were right to hand the match to Poll because he was a referee with great experience who knew how to handle a situation like that. Had there been someone of lesser experience refereeing the game, a penalty could easily have been awarded.

Our first chance fell to Paul Peschisolido, who was set up by Steve Howard, but his shot was comfortably saved by Dean Kiely. Craig Fagan was then narrowly off-target after cutting in from the right. The amount of work Craig does in games is incredible. He's a very unselfish player who'll play anywhere and he's a lovely lad as well.

Albion made quite a strong finish to the half with Koumas shooting just over the bar and then Kevin Phillips grazing the top of the bar with a 20-yard drive. They continued to apply some pressure after break with Bywater making a save from Koumas and Kamara putting a free-kick over the bar.

The gaffer made a change with the very talented teenager Giles Barnes, who had been thought to be out because of an injury he had picked up towards the end of the season, coming on in place of Peschisolido and we nearly scored soon afterwards. Matt Oakley got on the end of a cross from Fagan and only a good finger-tip save from Kiely kept the ball out.

We didn't have to wait long to score because Stephen Pearson grabbed what proved to be the winning goal moments later. Howard found Barnes whose low ball across the face of goal was fired home by Pearson. It was a great strike and what a time to score his first goal for the club!

As Albion looked for a quick response, Bywater was called into action to claim the ball at the second attempt following a shot from Gera. He also kept out a header from Robinson as Albion continued to press forward.

I thought that as long as we kept it tight and no-one did anything silly, we'd be all right. Everybody knew what they had to do, so as long as everyone kept doing their jobs properly, I didn't feel that we were going to concede. The work-rate and commitment was great and the lads handled the situation superbly. We put in a performance which justified our current status as a Premiership club.

It was a fabulous feeling at the end when the final whistle was blown. It was a great day for the fans. They believed we could do it and they got right behind us. The support they gave us throughout the season was excellent.

As I've said before, given my links with Albion, I'd rather have beaten another club to go up. I spoke to a few of the Albion players at the end because I wanted to show my respect for them. I wanted to let them know that they'd taken part in a great final. I told them that with the players they had, there was every reason for them to feel confident about winning promotion the following season. I also showed my appreciation to the Albion fans, who I still enjoy a good relationship with. They know me as a person and as a player and they know what I did for the club.

THE FACT THAT Billy Davies, with his passion and drive, managed to lead us back to the Premier League shouldn't have really surprised anyone. You only had to look at what he did in the previous season at Preston, taking them to the play-off semi-finals. He's a very astute manager who gets his teams to play with passion and desire.

I've already mentioned Stephen Bywater's impressive performances over the course of the season and my other defensive colleagues at Wembley also deserve praise. Tyrone Mears at right-back is a tremendous athlete who's very quick. He's a player who's destined to go all the way to the very top and win international honours. That's how highly I regard him. Tyrone and 'Fages' [Craig Fagan] did ever so well on the right-hand side because I thought Jason Koumas and Paul Robinson would be dangerous. The way Tyrone and Fages started, snuffing out the danger from those two, won us the game. Koumas in particular can be very dangerous as he is so skilful on the ball and has a good shot from distance, but they managed to keep him quiet.

Jay McEveley, who signed before the deadline in January from Blackburn, is a young left-back with a lot of quality. He's got bags of potential so he'll get better and better as the years go by. Dean Leacock was a magnificent signing from Fulham. He's a young player who's calm and composed on the ball while being very tenacious. I enjoy playing alongside 'Deano'. He listens and learns and he'll get better and better. Playing in the Premiership will stand him in good stead.

I'd also like to say a few words about my Jamaica team-mate Michael Johnson, who didn't feature at Wembley, because he's a great pro who's been around for a long time. 'Johnno' is a great competitor, as well as being a joker in the dressing room. You know exactly what you're going to get from him when he goes out on the pitch, week in, week out and that's why he's still playing now. I can't miss out Mo Kamara because he did ever so well at the start of the season. He's a very steady player with lots of experience.

Matt Oakley has been a great captain because he's very calm and composed and says the right thing at the right time, which is what you need from your captain. He's a clever player who is a great inspiration in his play and he scored some vital goals for us that season. The gaffer deserves praise for bringing him in.

The match-winner at Wembley, Stephen Pearson, has the nick-name 'Road Runner' because he's got a great engine and he covers every blade of grass. Seth Johnson played a pivotal role in our success at Wembley.

He's got great passing ability and he's also a good tackler. Seth cost Leeds £9million and you don't play for England like he did if you're not a good player. He was exactly what we needed when he came to the club. Seth picked up an injury in the Play-off final and it's a shame that he's had so many problems with injuries because he's definitely got the ability to play at the level we're at today, without a doubt. If it wasn't for his injury problems, I'm sure he'd still be here, playing a huge role for us in midfield. Seth's another joker and we miss him in the dressing room.

Up front, we had Stevie Howard and Paul Peschisolido, who were magnificent. The gaffer paid £1million to sign Stevie from Luton and a lot of people were questioning the size of the fee, but he scored 19 goals and was an immense figure throughout the season. He offers incredible commitment and he's got his just rewards because here he is now in the Premier League, getting a chance to play against his boyhood team, Newcastle.

'Pesch' did ever so well that season, scoring some vital goals. Even though he's 36 now, he's still very fit and still has the ability to score goals. He's a busy, clever player who caused West Brom some problems. Pesch is a great lad and we spent a lot of time together because we both live in Birmingham, so we used to drive together to Derby. It's a friendship which will last beyond football. He's still in contact with a lot of the lads at the club which just goes to show what type of person he is.

Giles Barnes came on at Wembley and changed the game for us in a ten-minute spell when we got the goal. He's got the potential to go all the way to the top because with his pace and power, he's the type of player managers are looking for in today's game. He's a very exciting player and a confident lad. It's just unfortunate that he's been hampered by injury. We're looking forward to him having a good run of games now.

Billy Davies brought in a number of new staff over the summer to help him. David Kelly came in as the gaffer's assistant and there's a new fitness coach called John Ireland. It's great to have them on board because they're all great guys and they can help us to move forward.

At the start of the 2007/08 season, I played in the first three games, against Portsmouth, Manchester City and Tottenham. Unfortunately, I then picked up an injury the night before the Liverpool game. After playing in a reserve game, I started training again, but then broke down with the same injury. I've been trying to come back ahead of schedule and it's been stop-start. Hopefully I can come back now and stay back.

It was always going to be a difficult season, but as the games go by we're getting used to the quickness of play. Kenny Miller has been a superb signing, scoring two goals in his first four games.

I DON'T KNOW WHAT the future holds. The only person who can answer that at this moment in time is God himself because he obviously sees the picture. I'd like to think that I could stay in football in some capacity. At the moment, it's kind of hard to think about life after football because I still enjoy playing so much and I'm just soaking up every moment as a player. I've done my 'A' and 'B' licences in coaching and I've taken a part-degree in PE, so there are plenty of avenues for me to go down and I'm keeping my options open.

My faith has been very, very important to me, ever since I was at Bradford. I came to know the Lord around the 1999/2000 period and since then my faith has been a very important part of my life. I enjoy going to church and I enjoy learning. There's so much pressure in football today, with a win-at-all-costs approach. Managers are now in a job for an average of 11-17 months, which is quite incredible. It just goes to show that it's a highly pressurised and I find that my faith gives me peace within. I am at peace on and off the pitch and that has made me a stronger, more positive character, which is good for me personally and the team. In sport, you need that positive vibe because it can give you the edge over the opposition. Of course, even when my football career finishes, my faith will continue to play a pivotal part in my life in general.